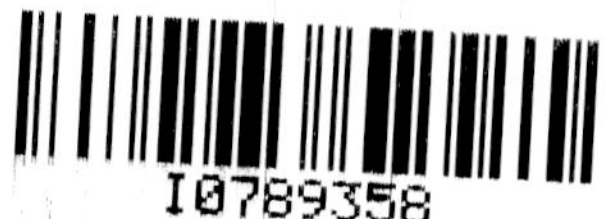

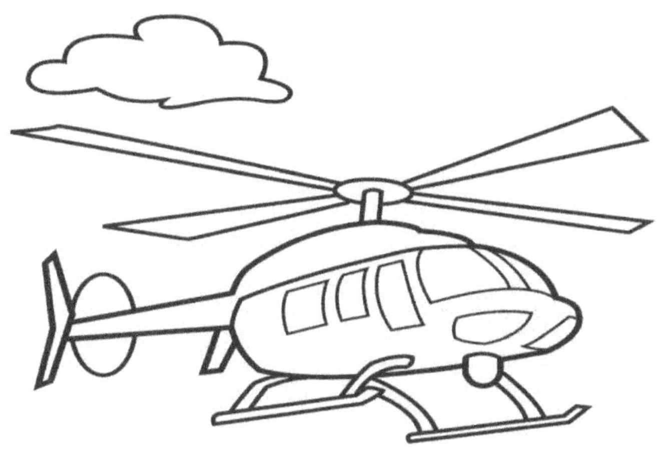

This Coloring Book
Belongs to :

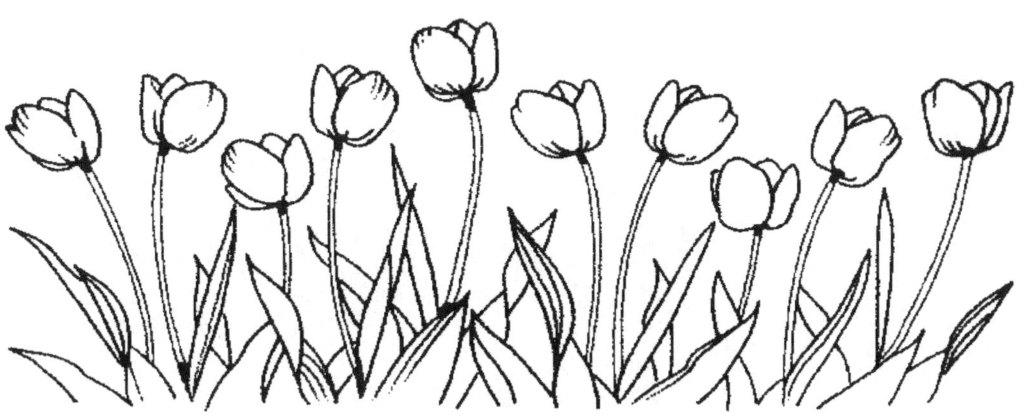

ENJOY!

8,5 . 11 inch | 100 pages

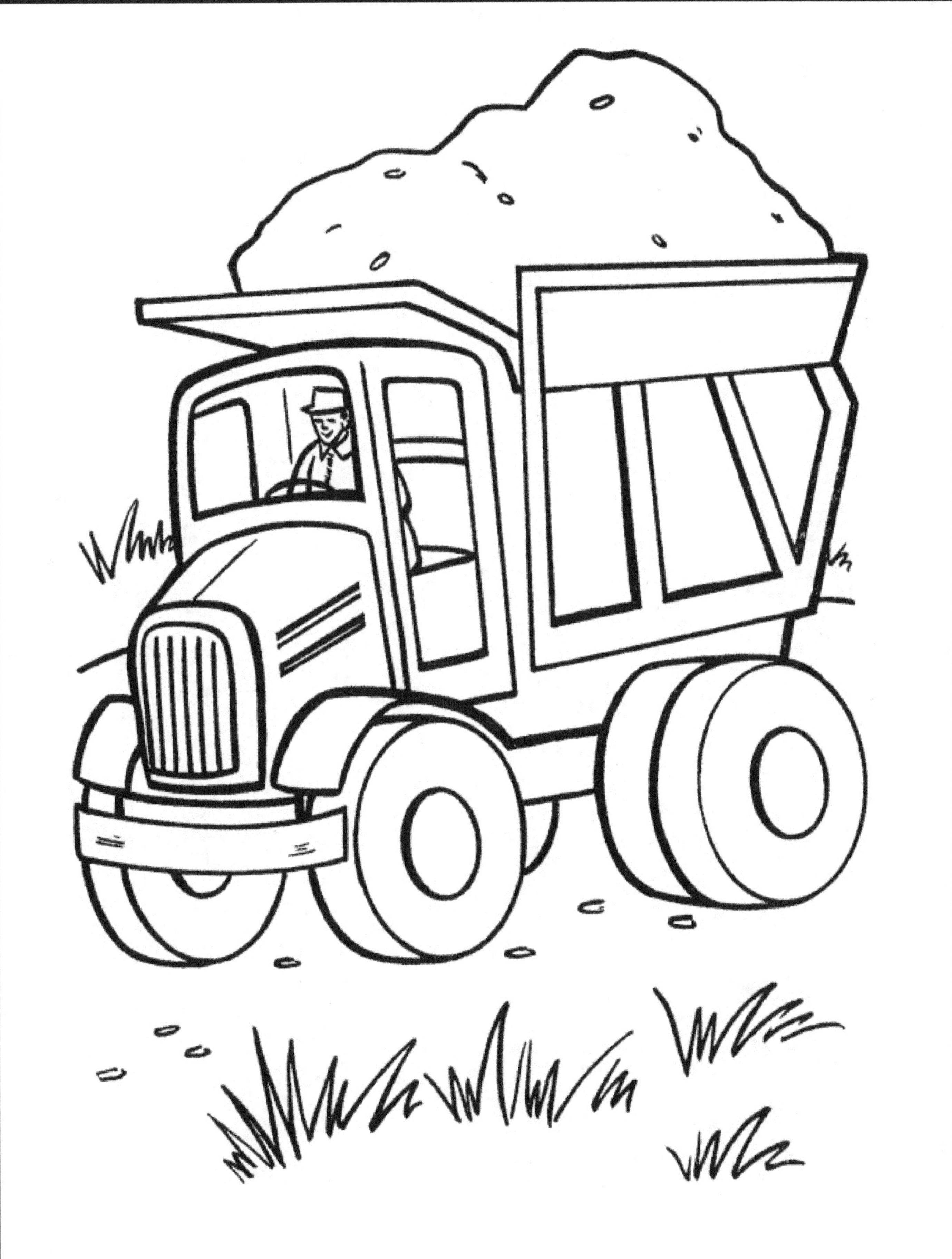

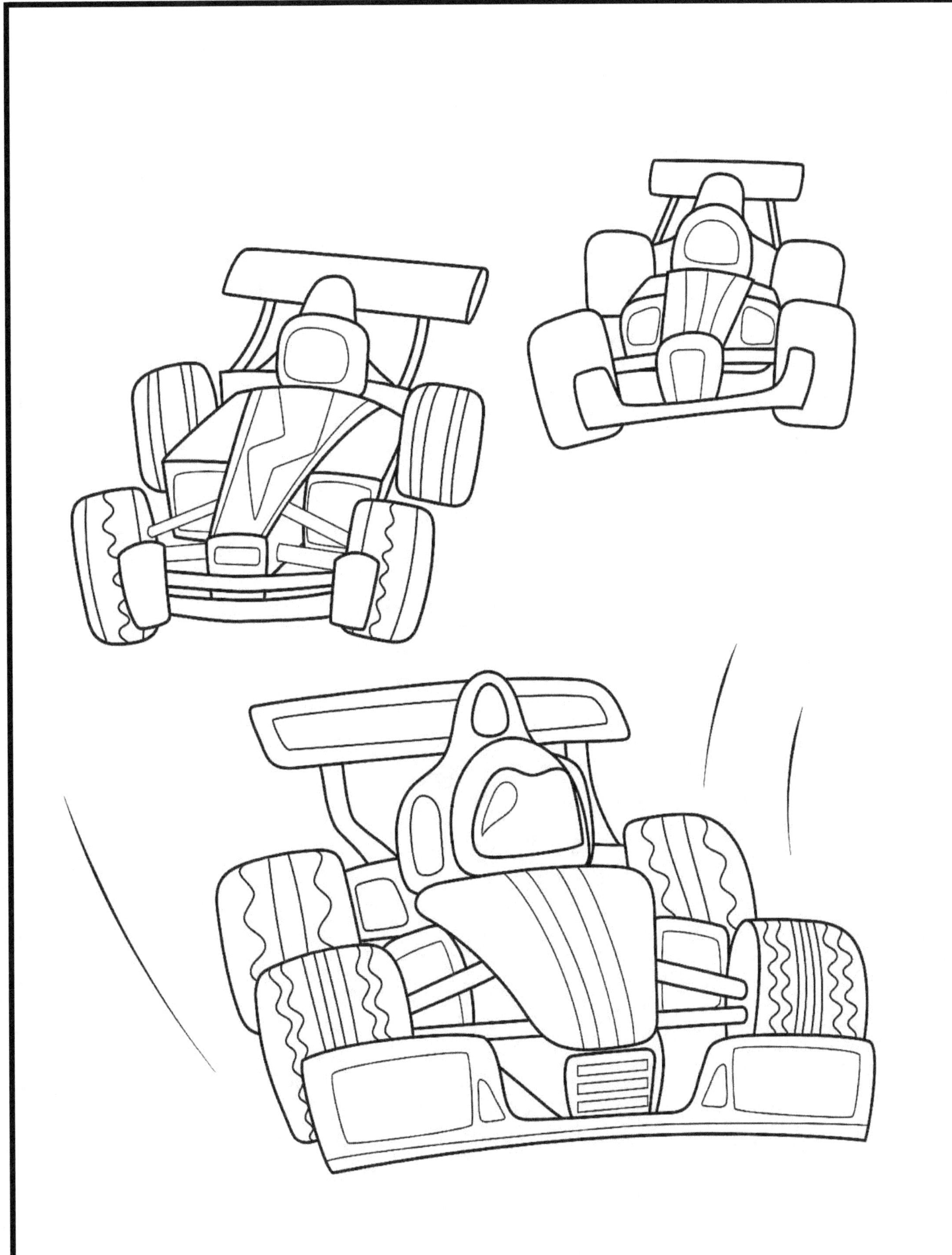

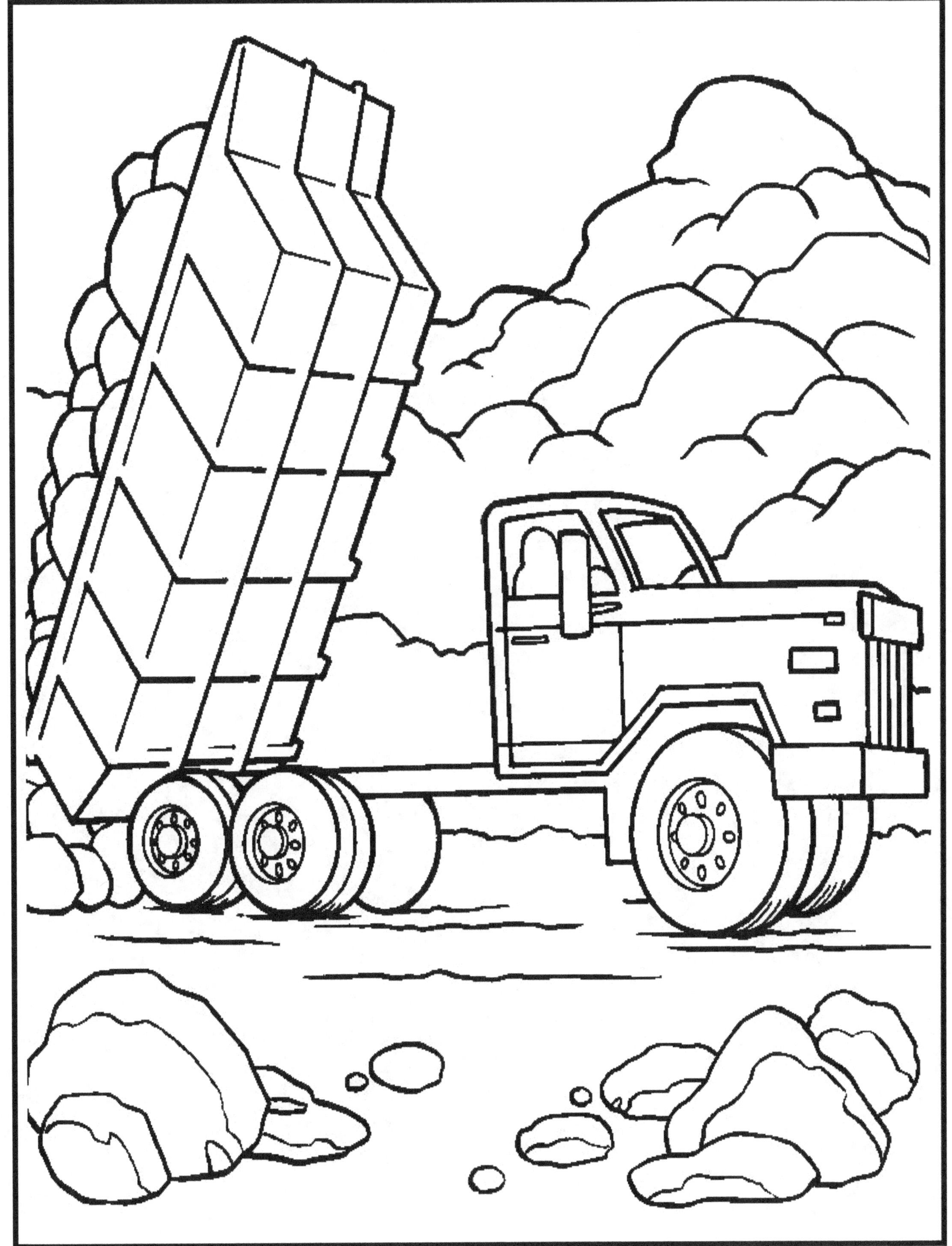

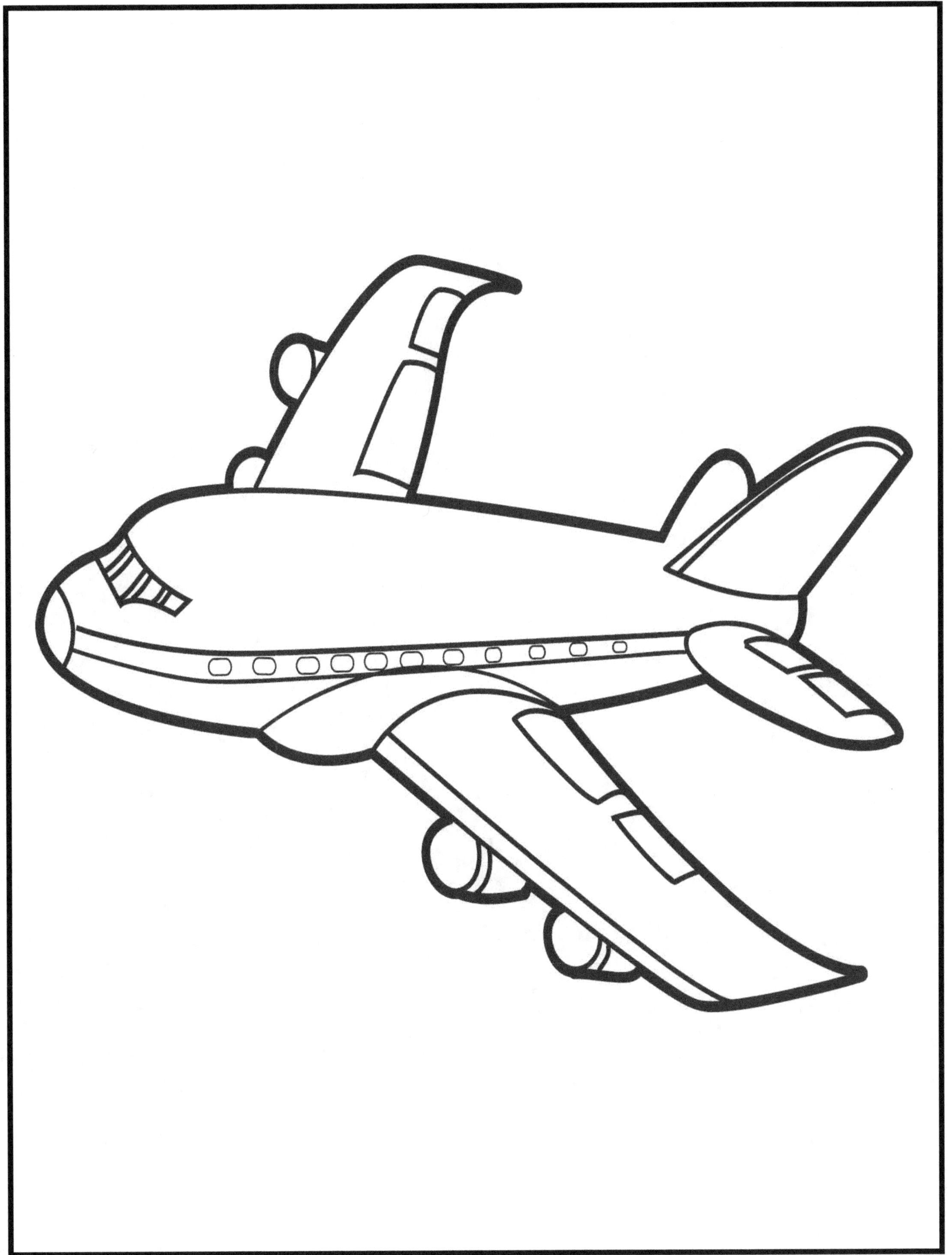

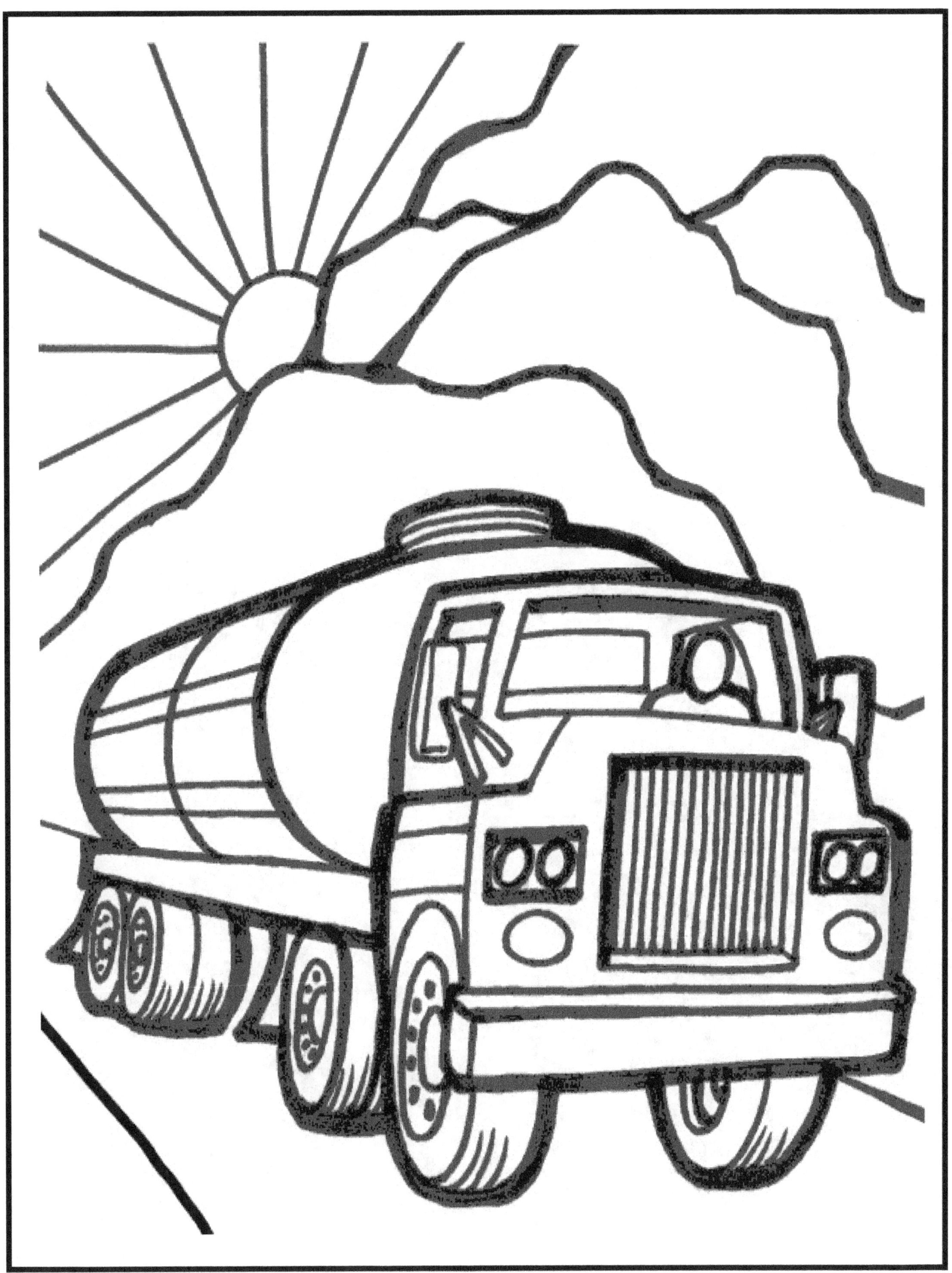

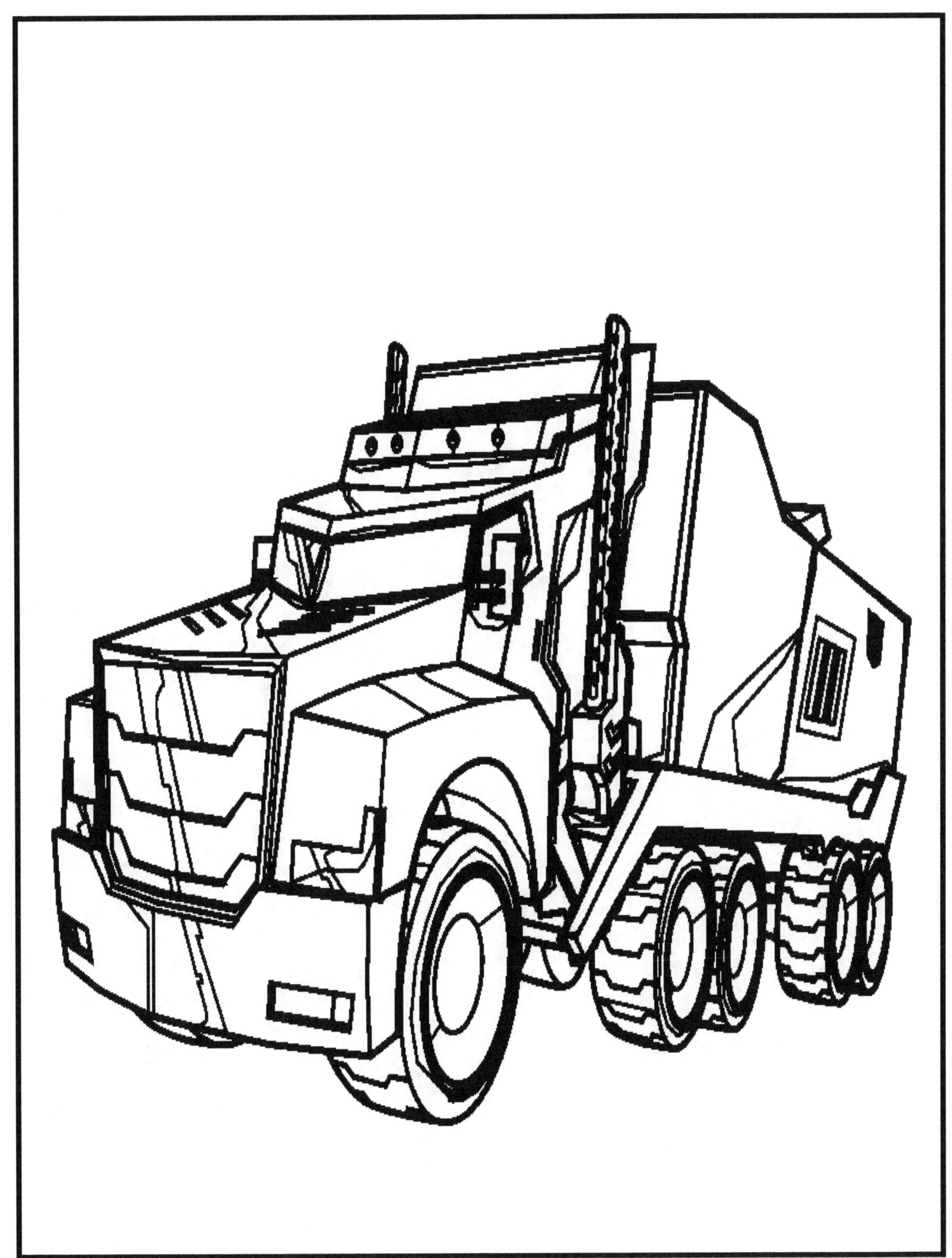

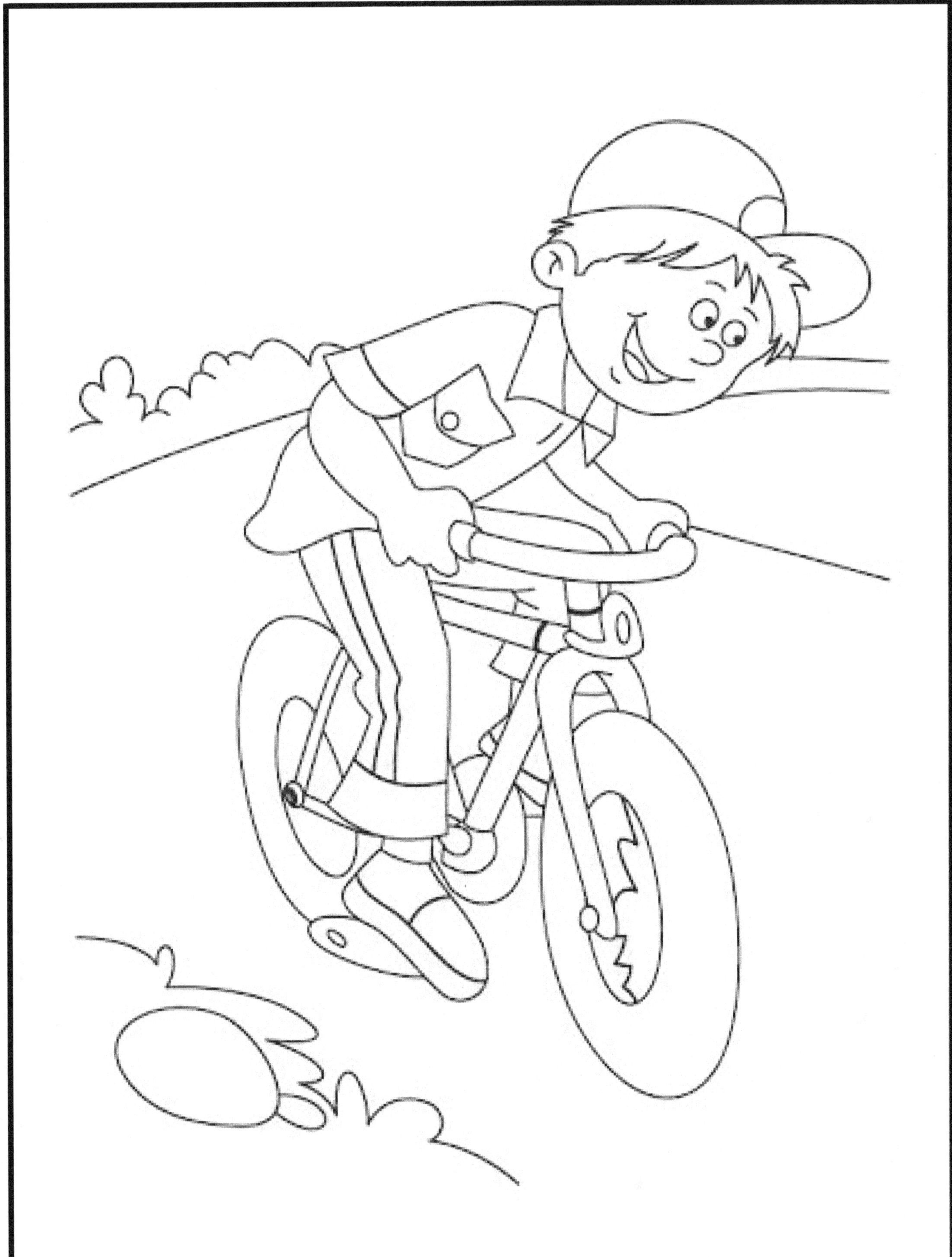

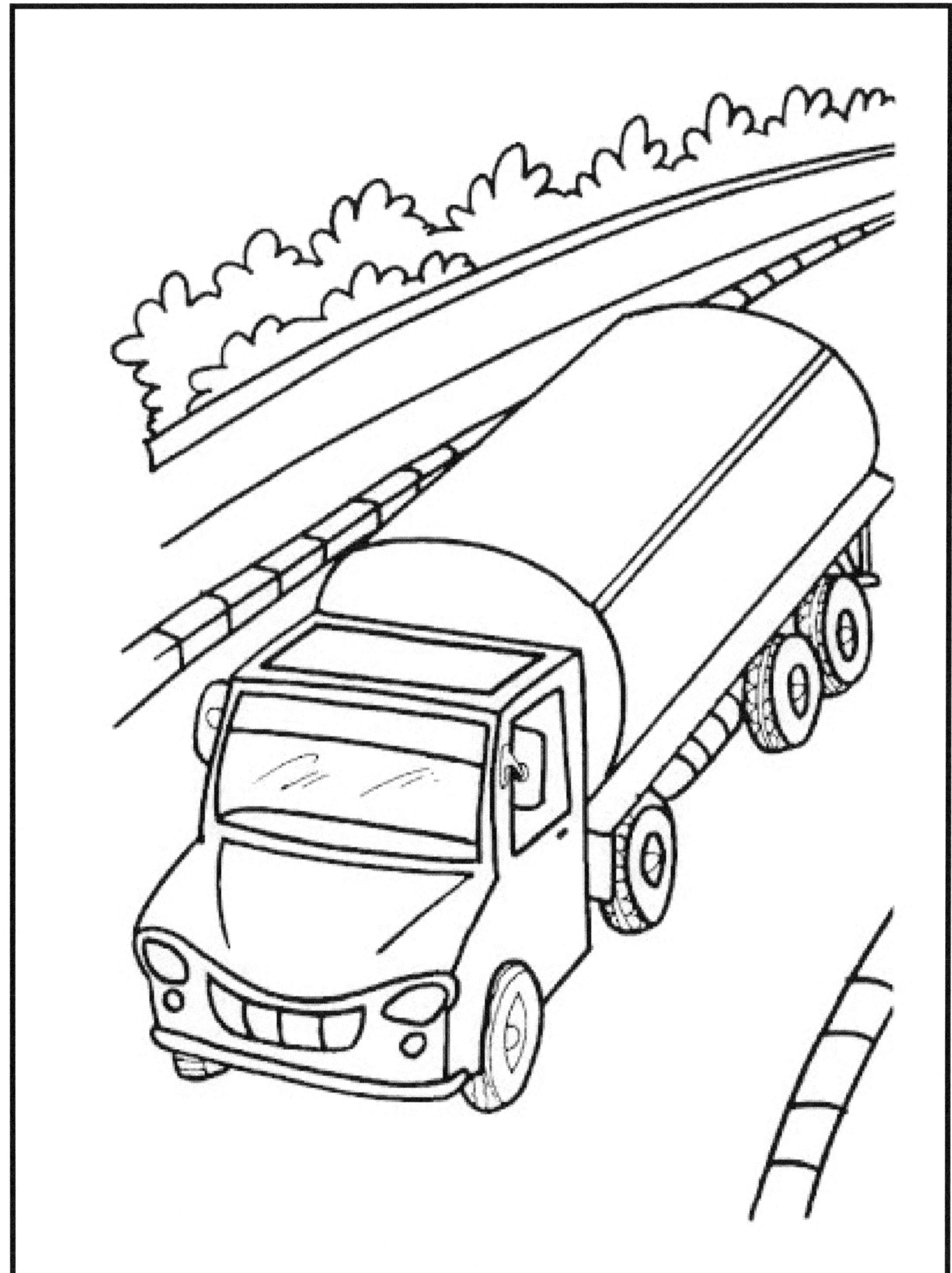

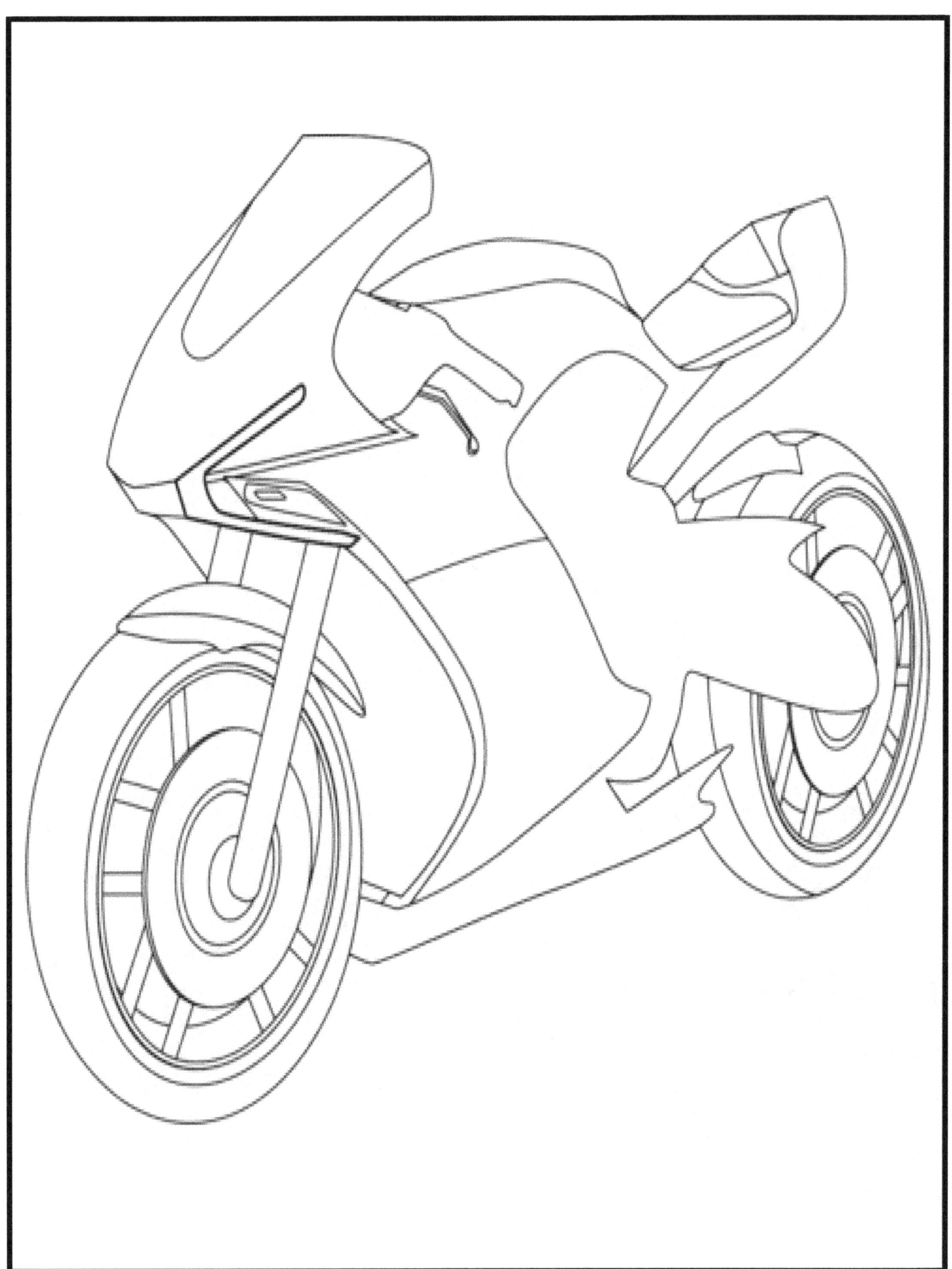

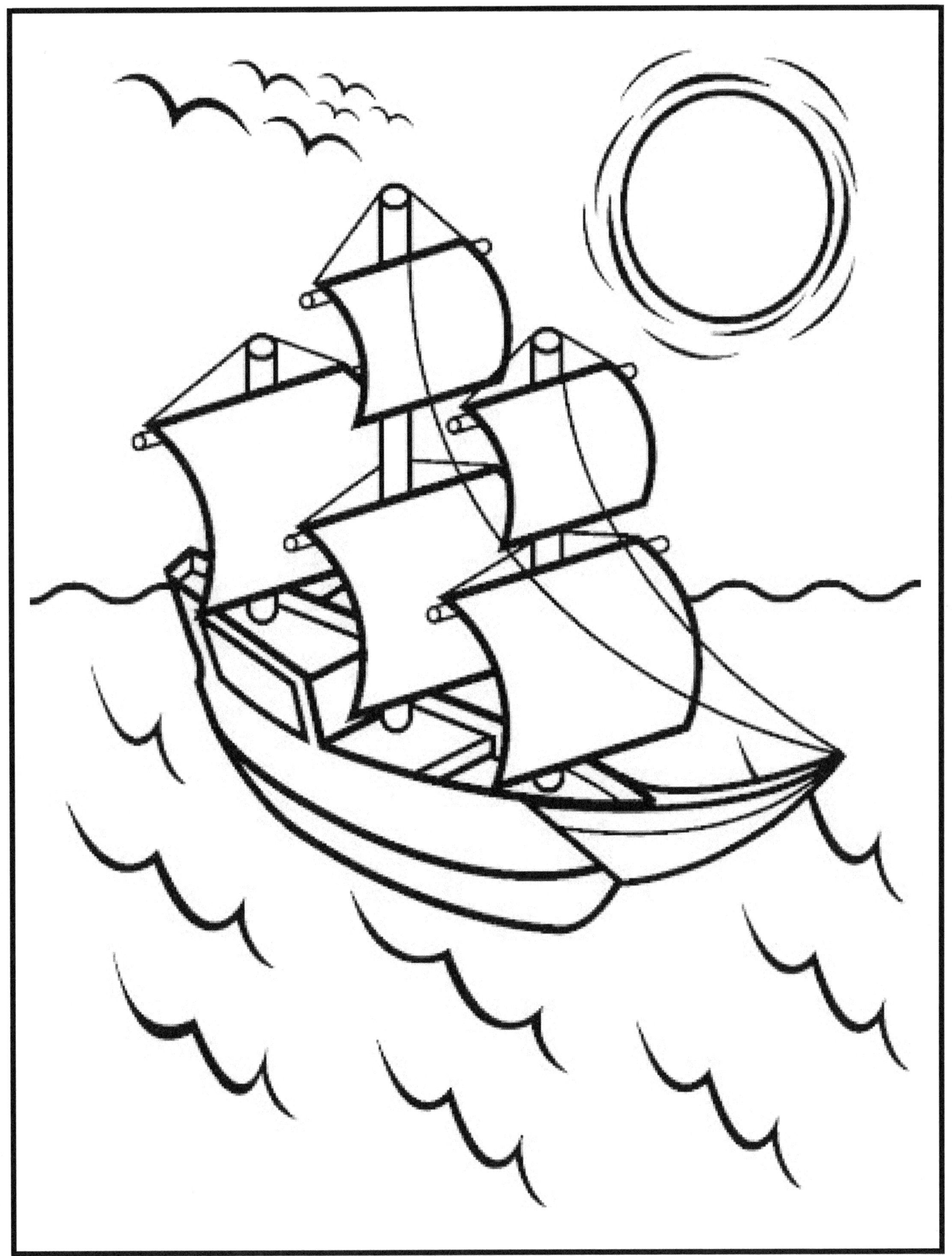

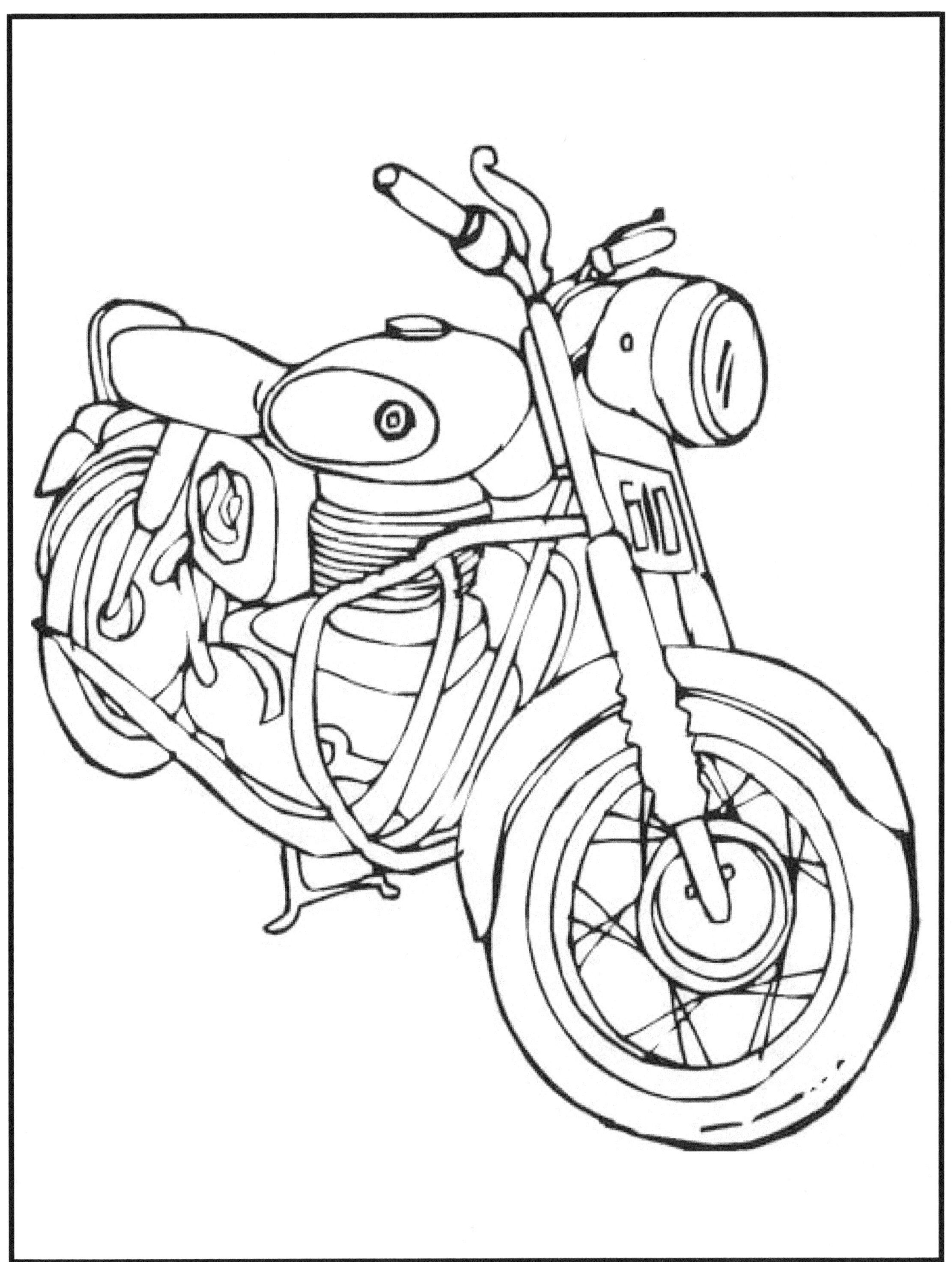

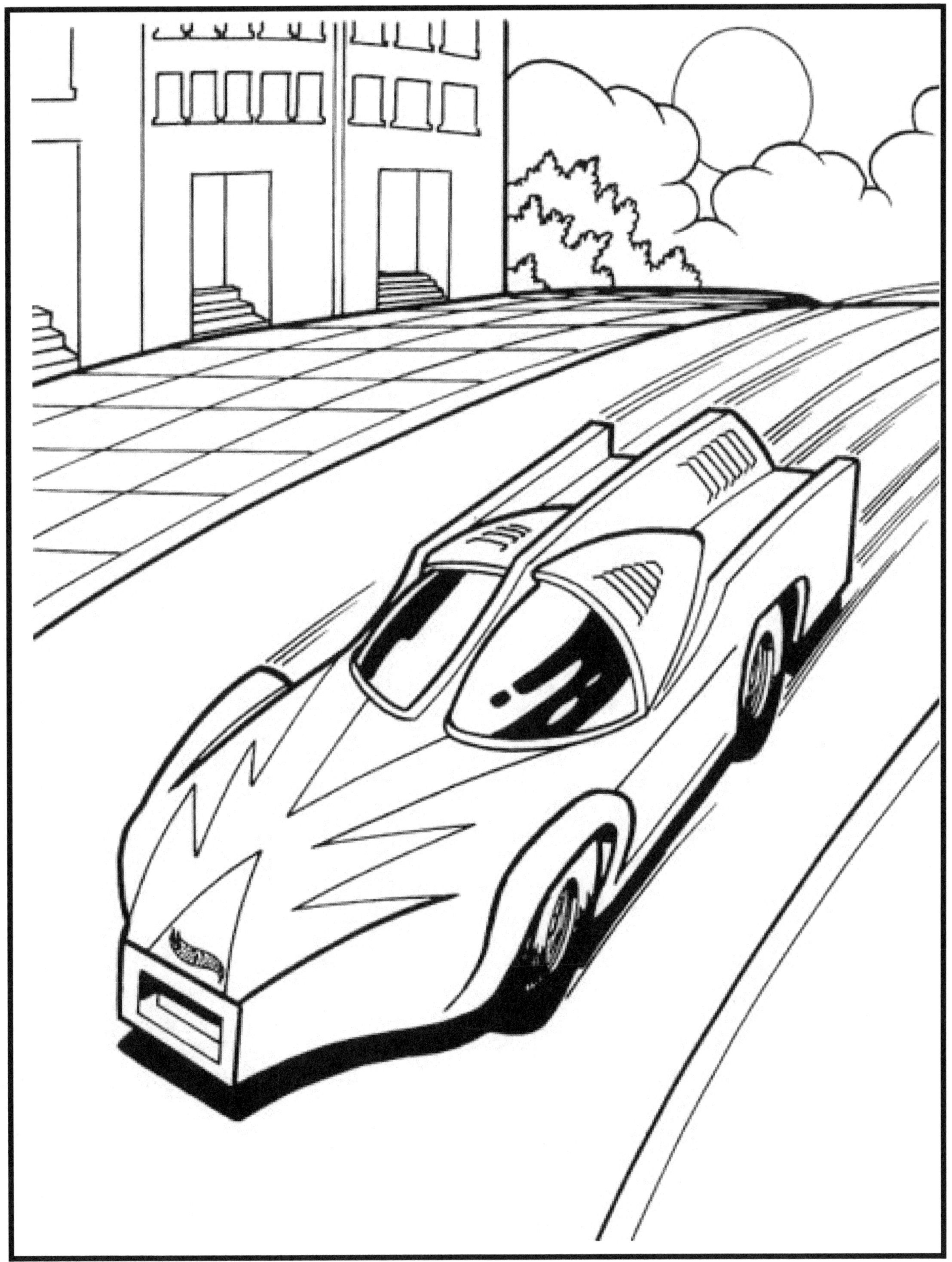

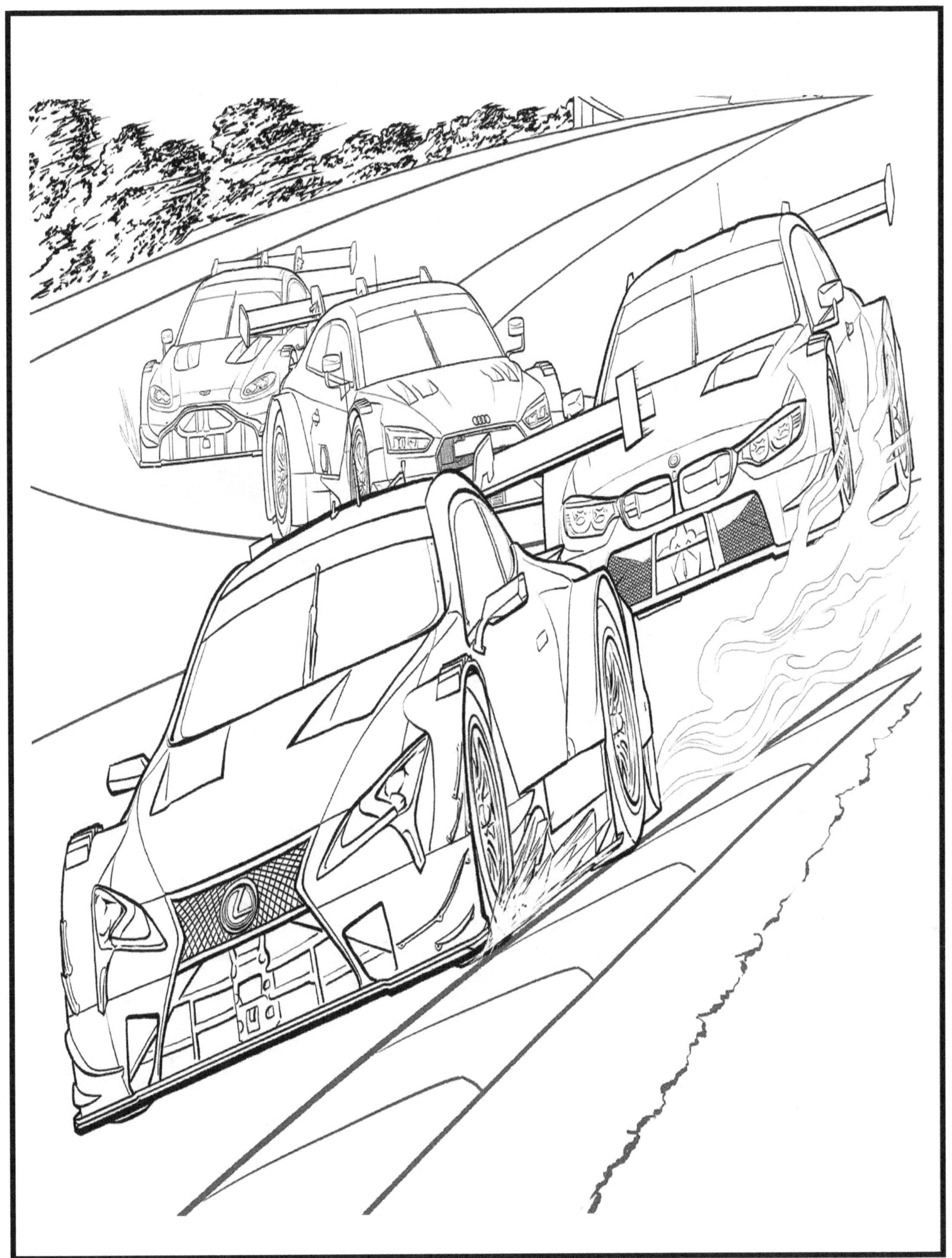

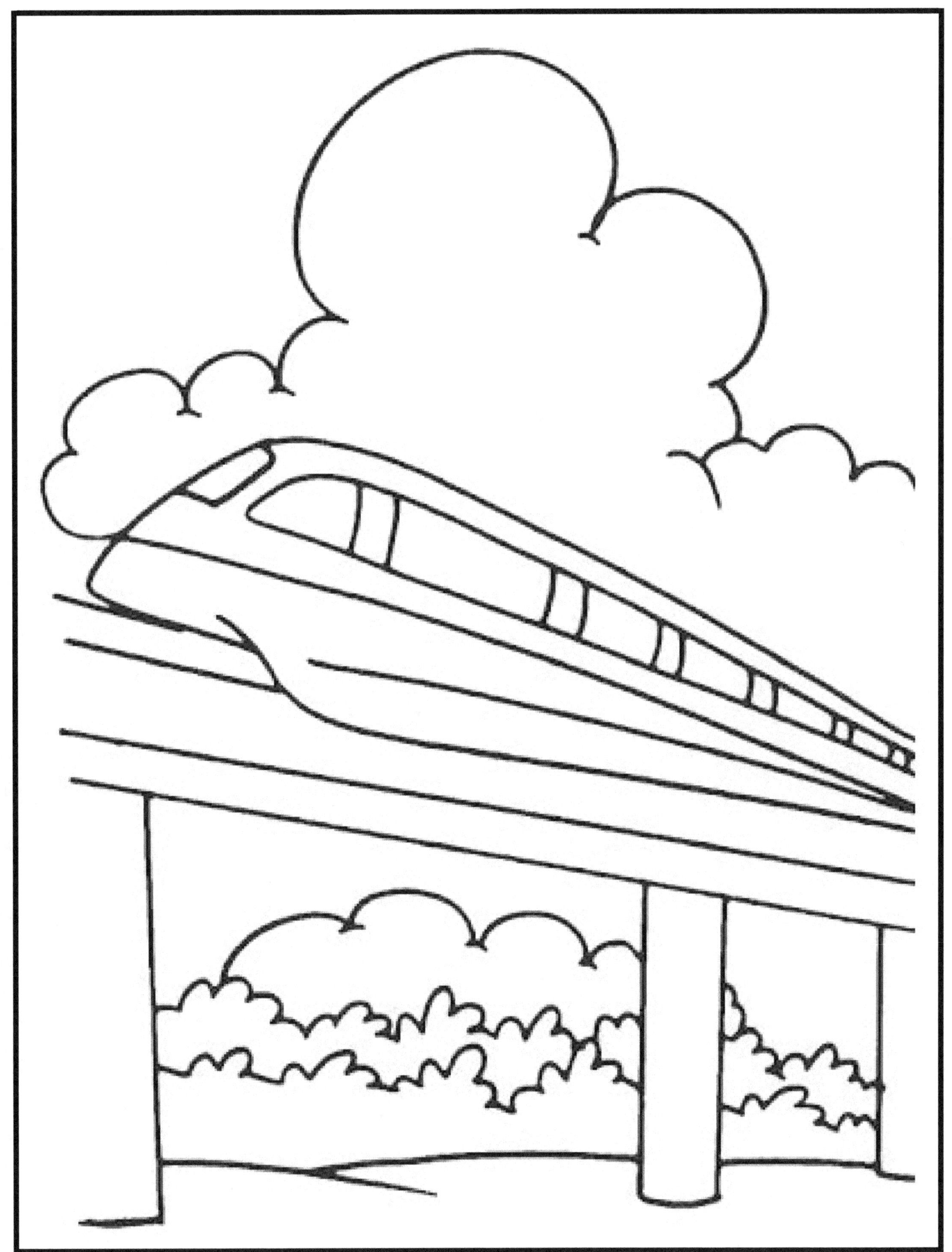

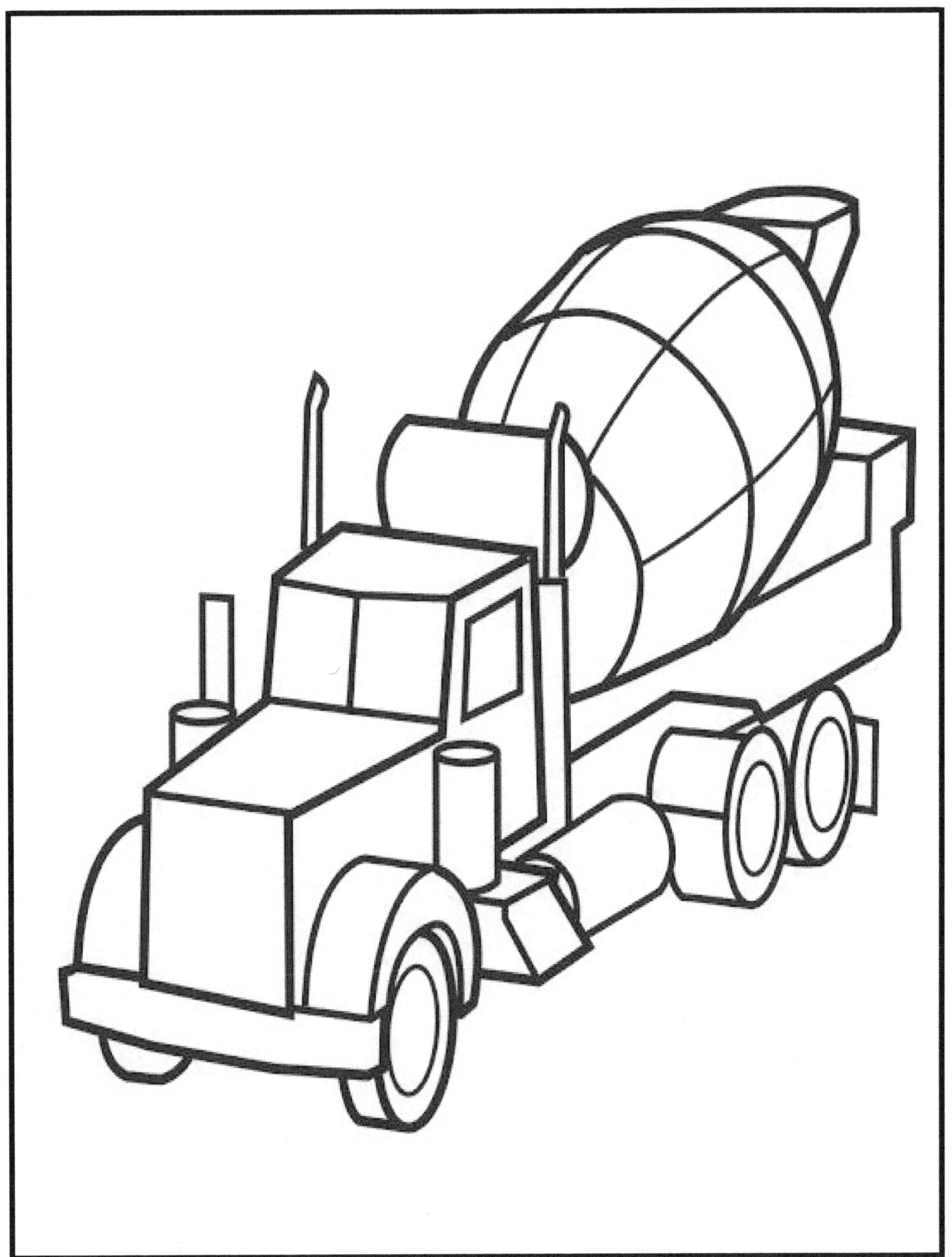

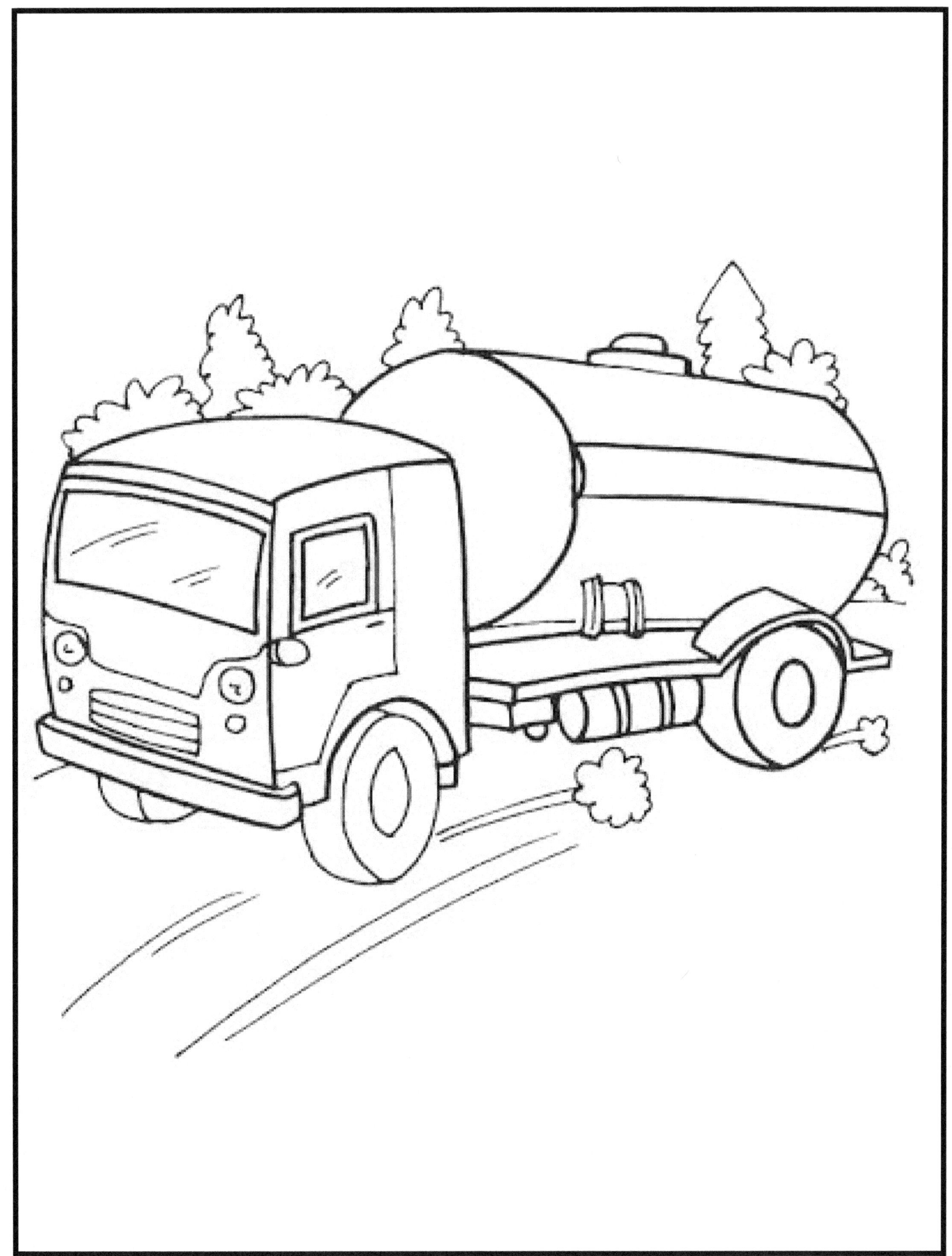

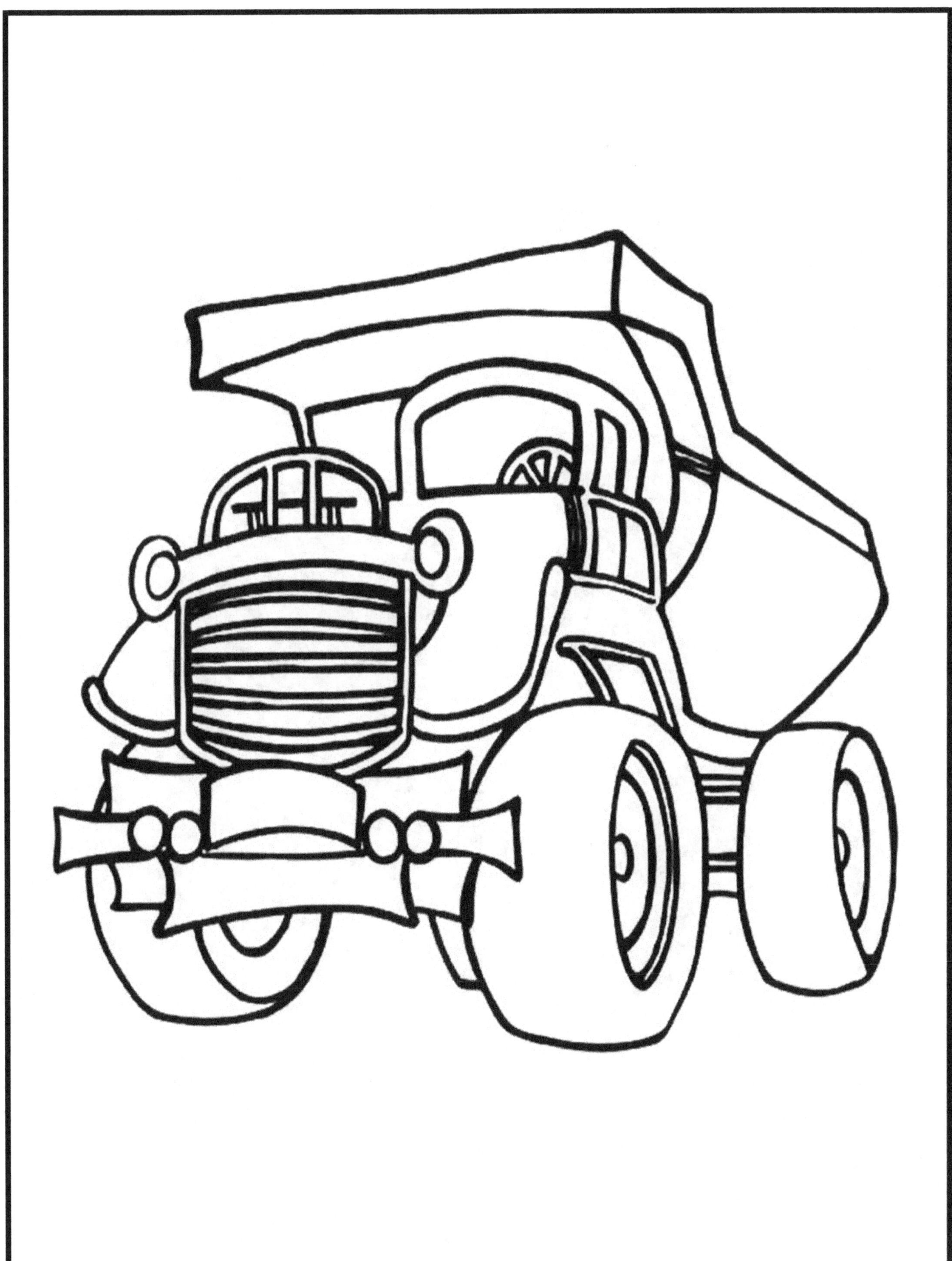

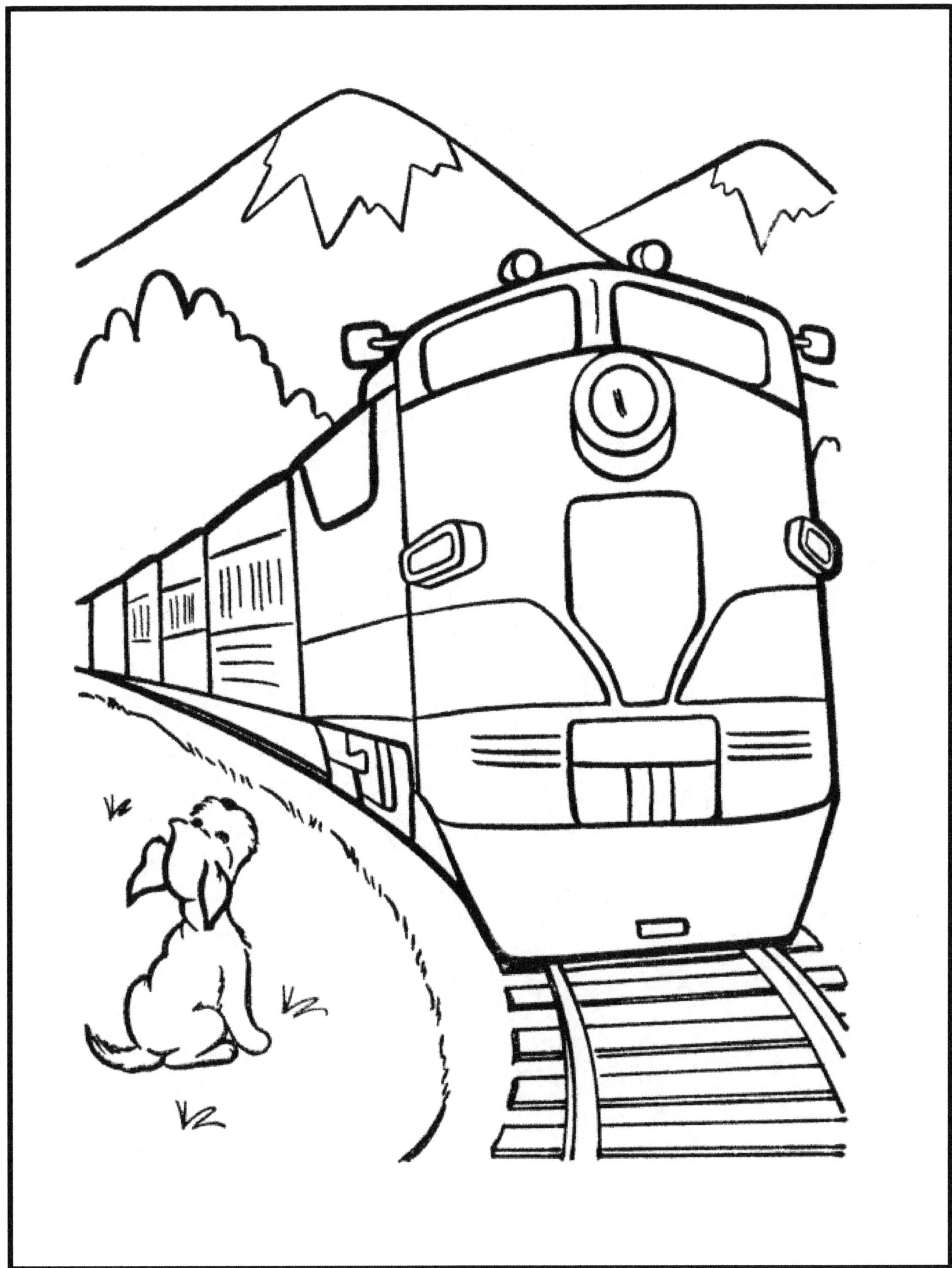

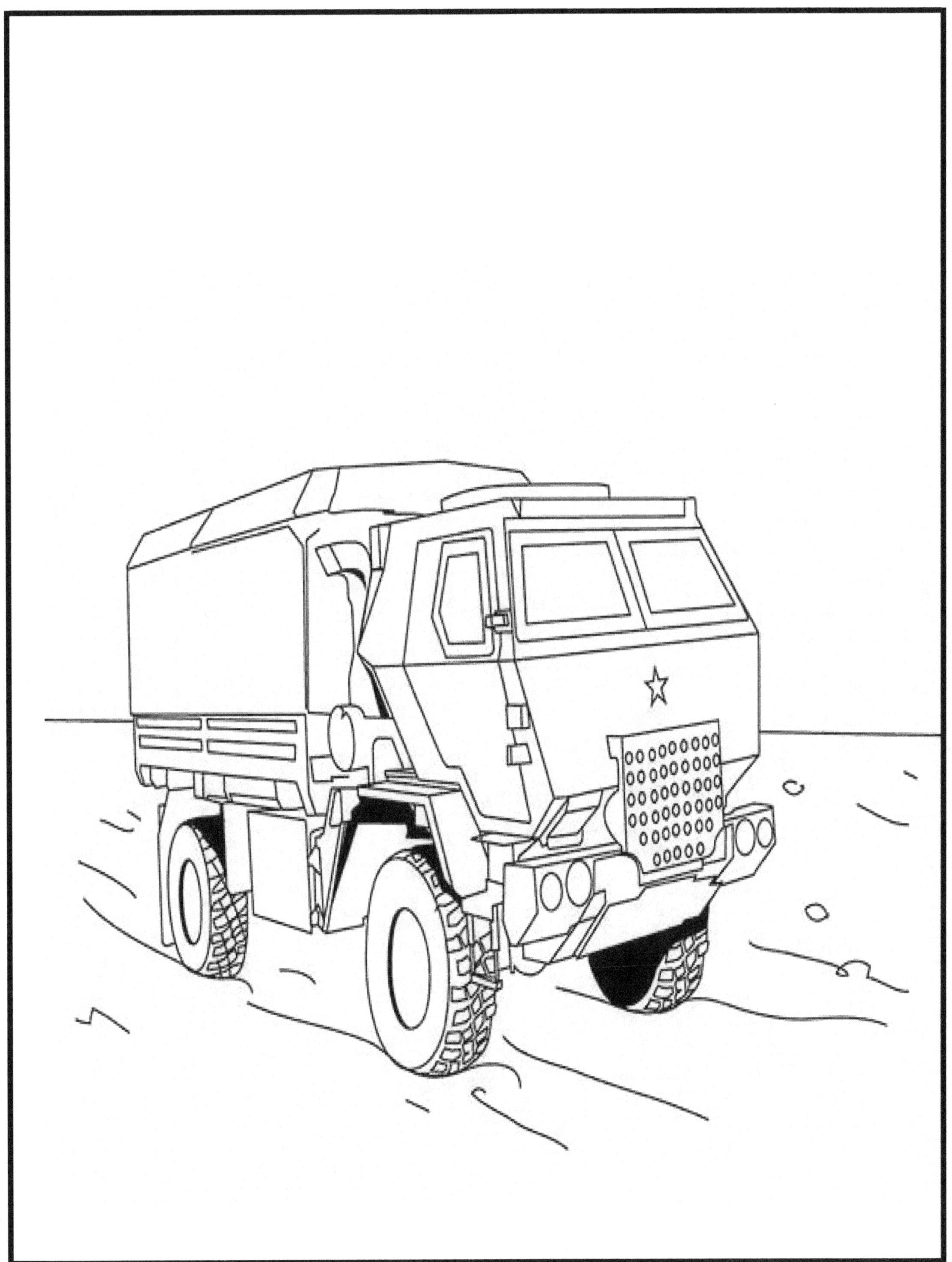

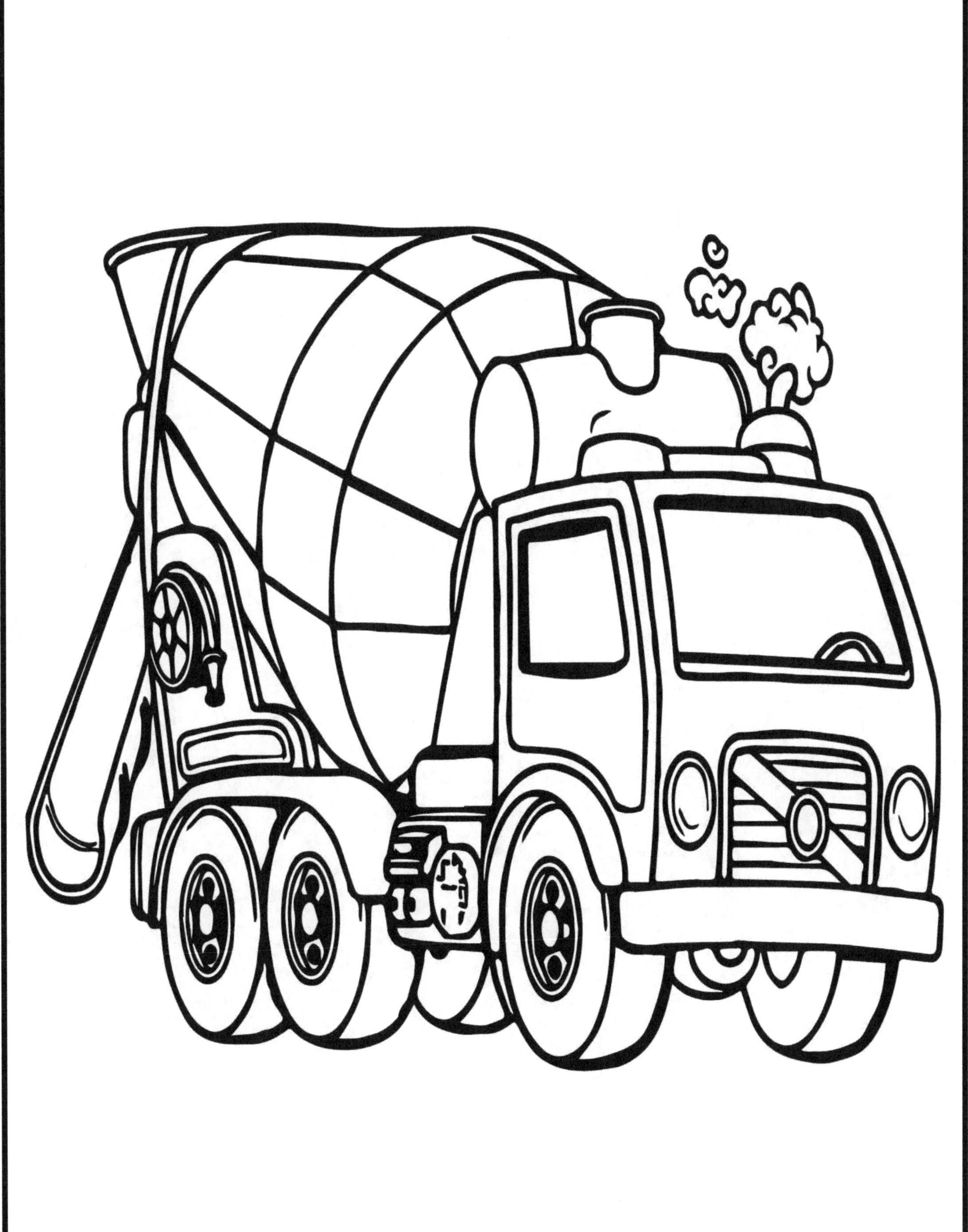

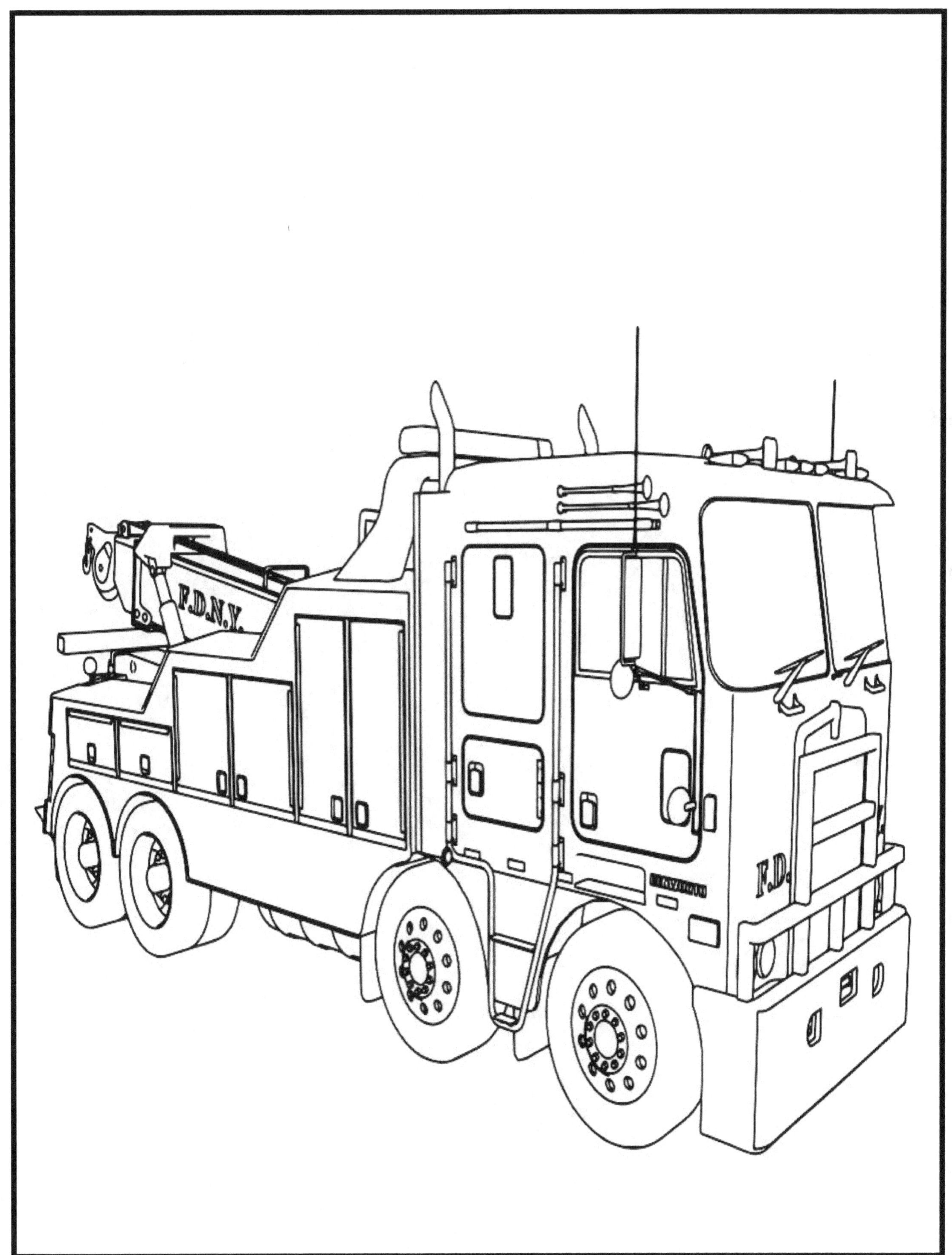

F.D.N.Y.
F.D.

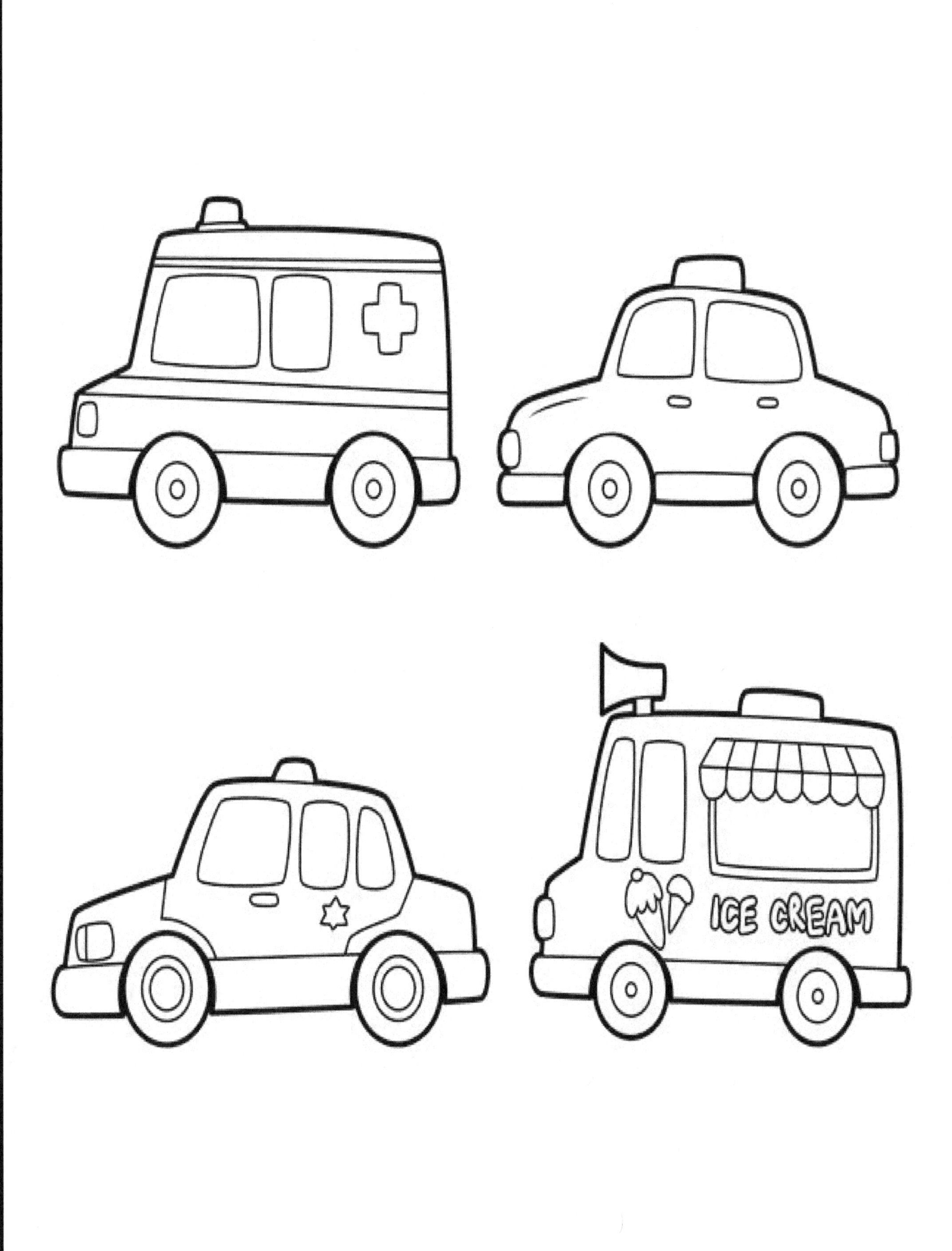
ICE CREAM

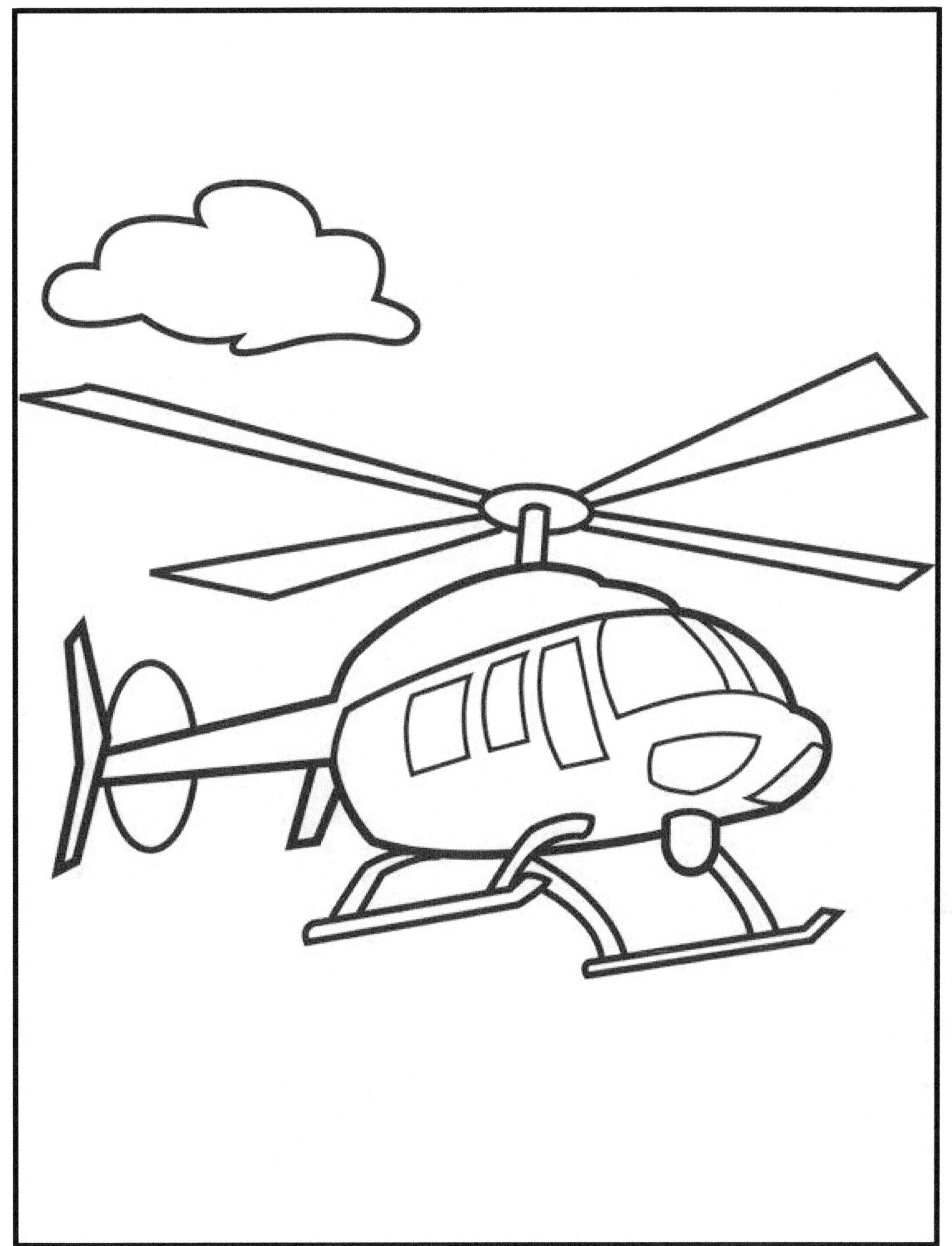

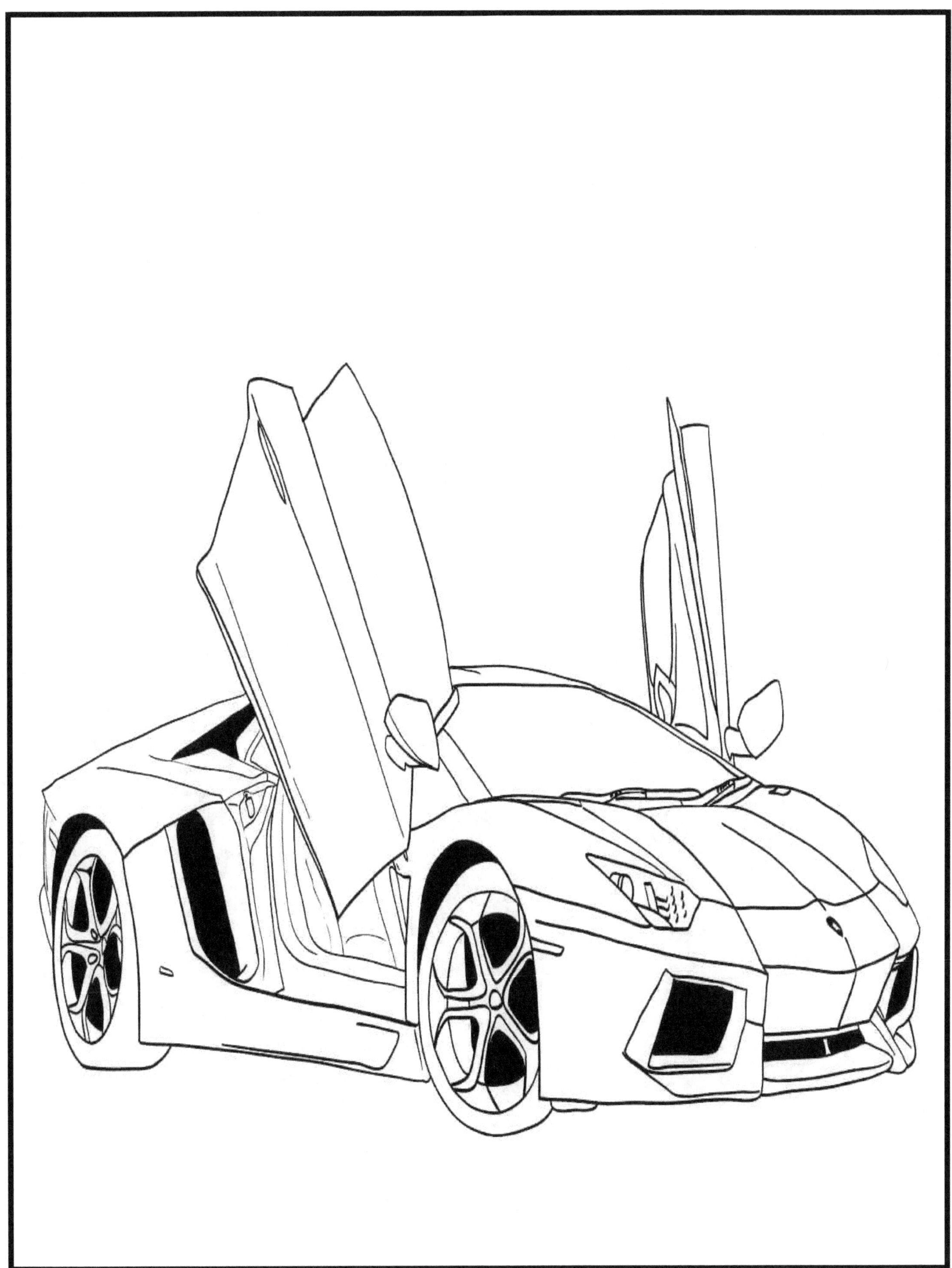

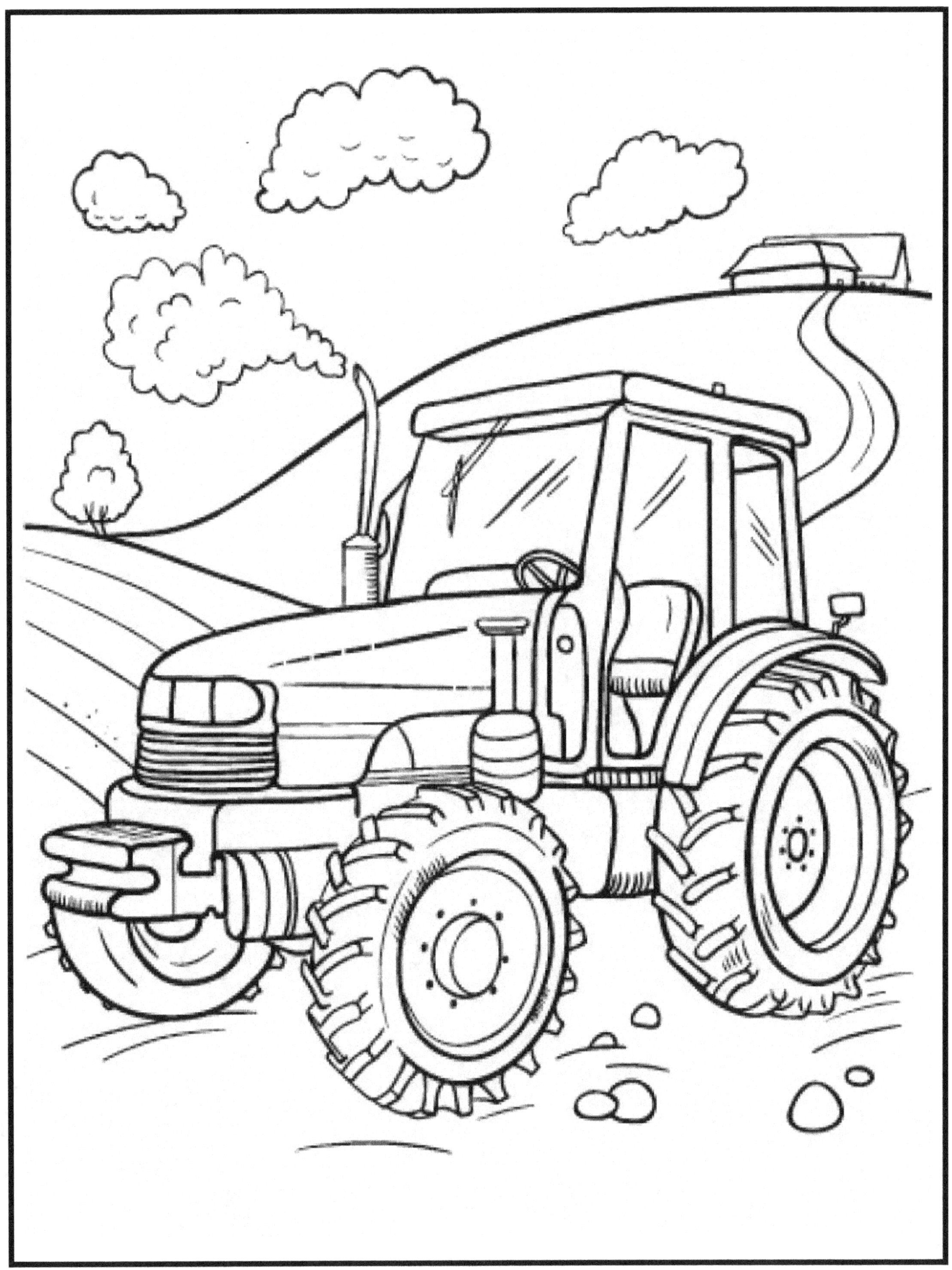

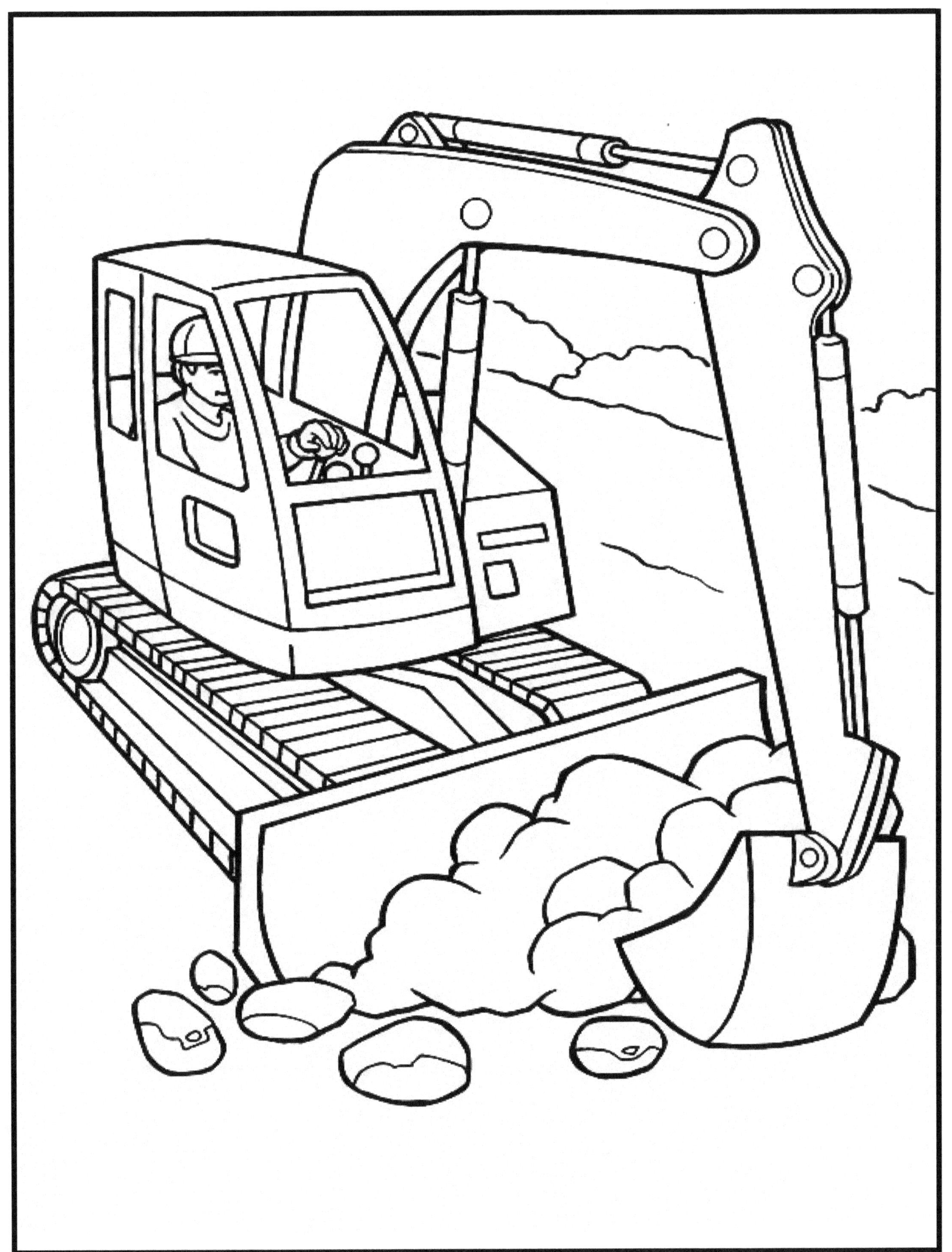

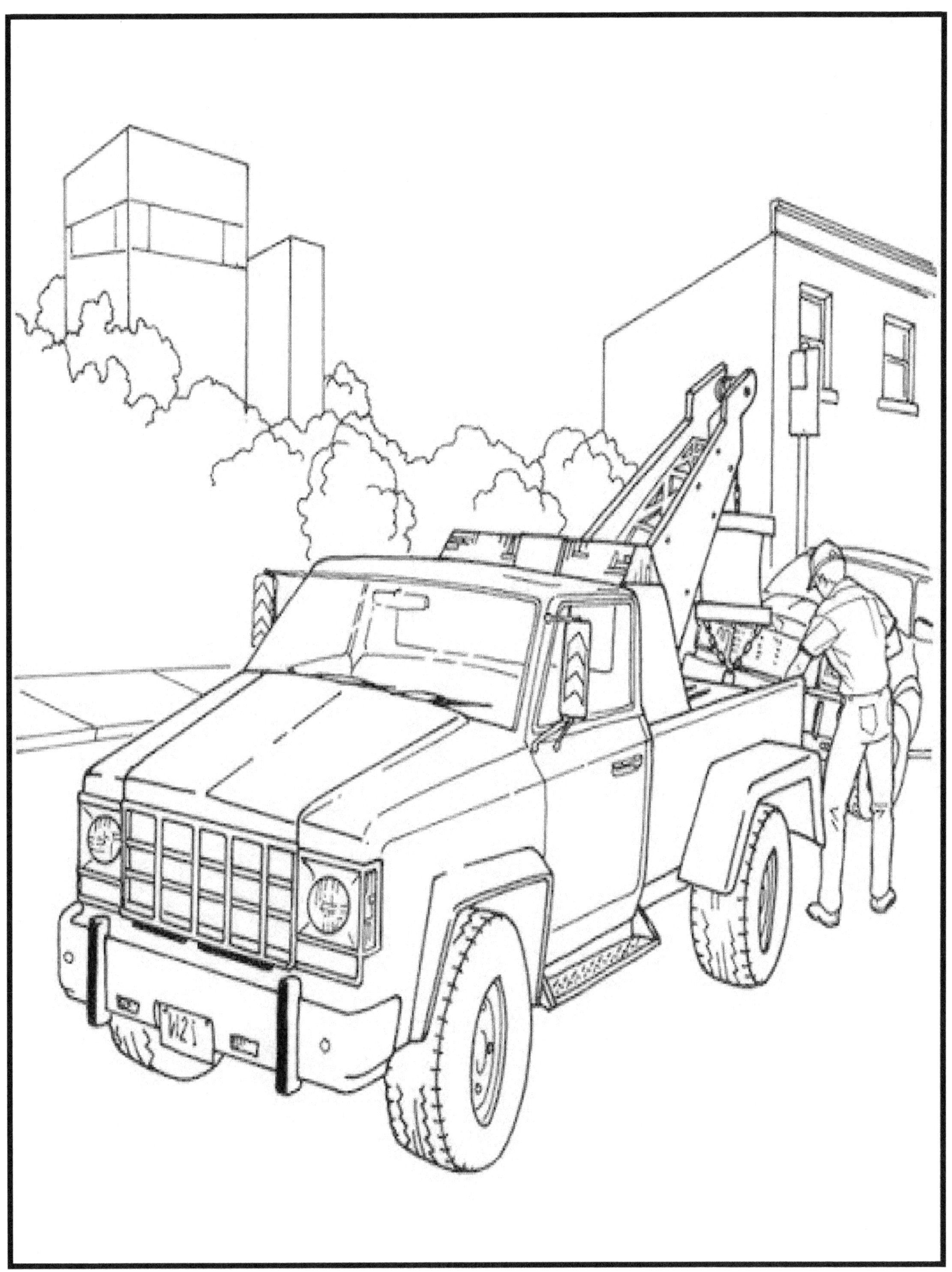

W21

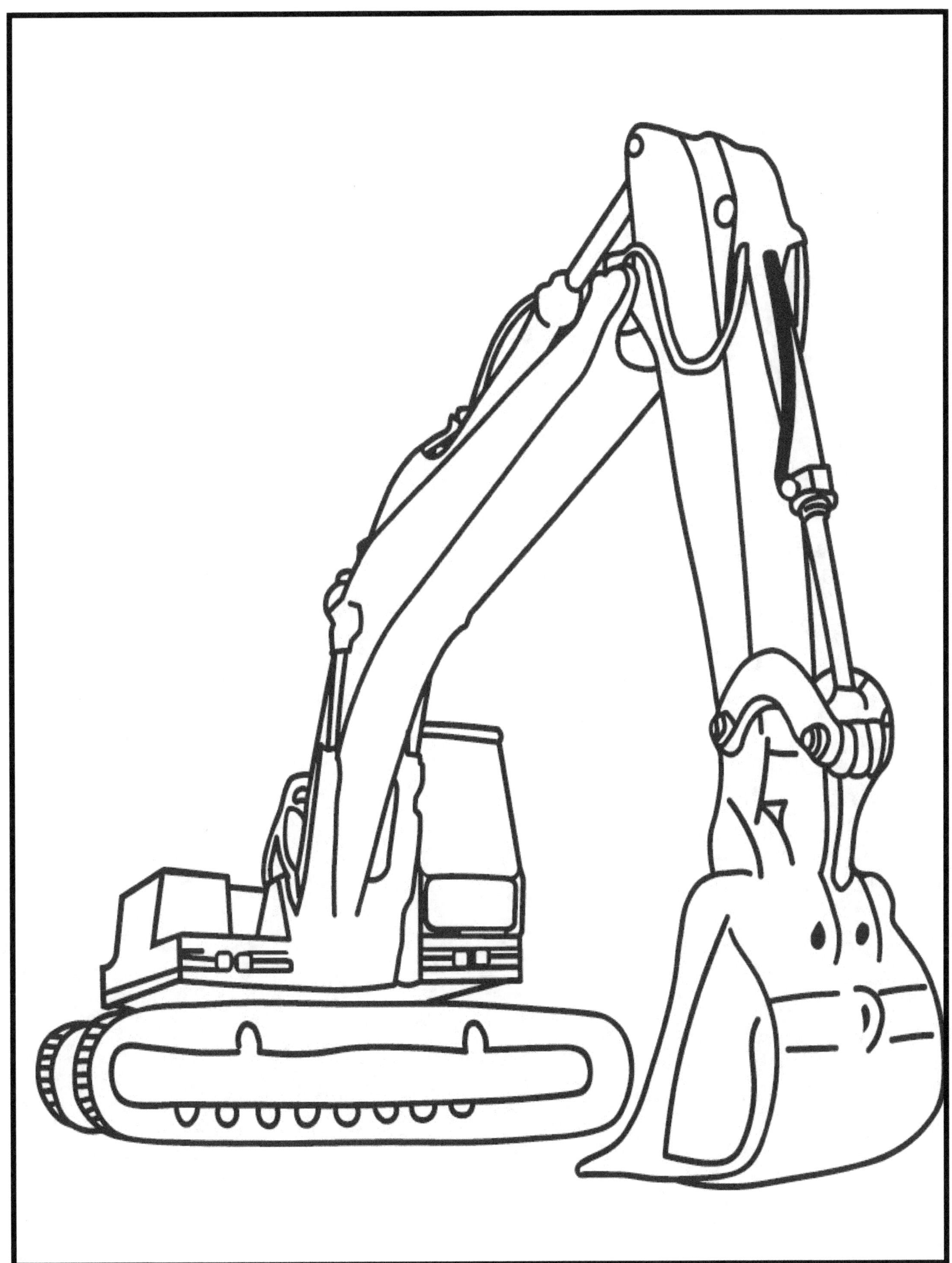

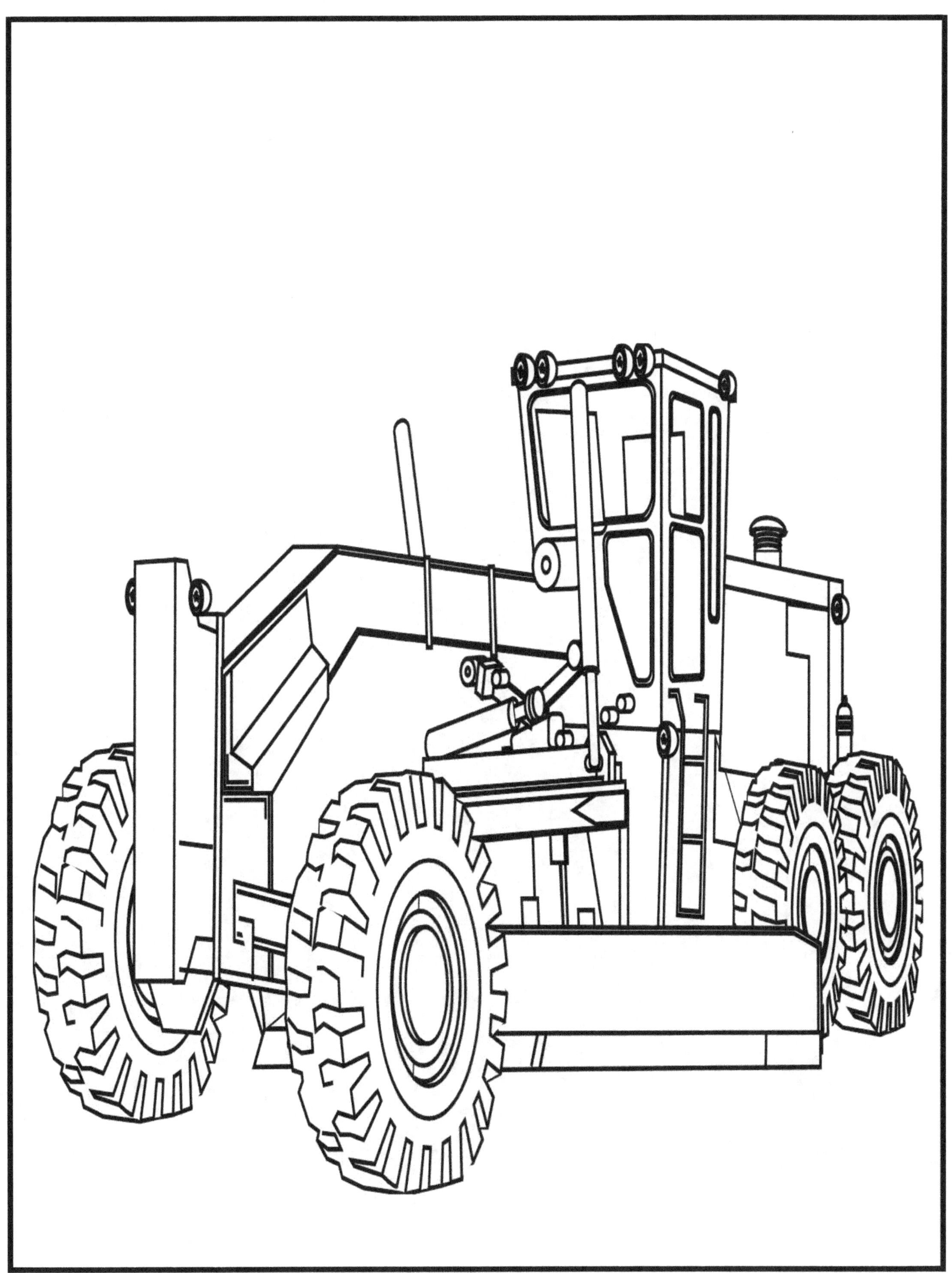

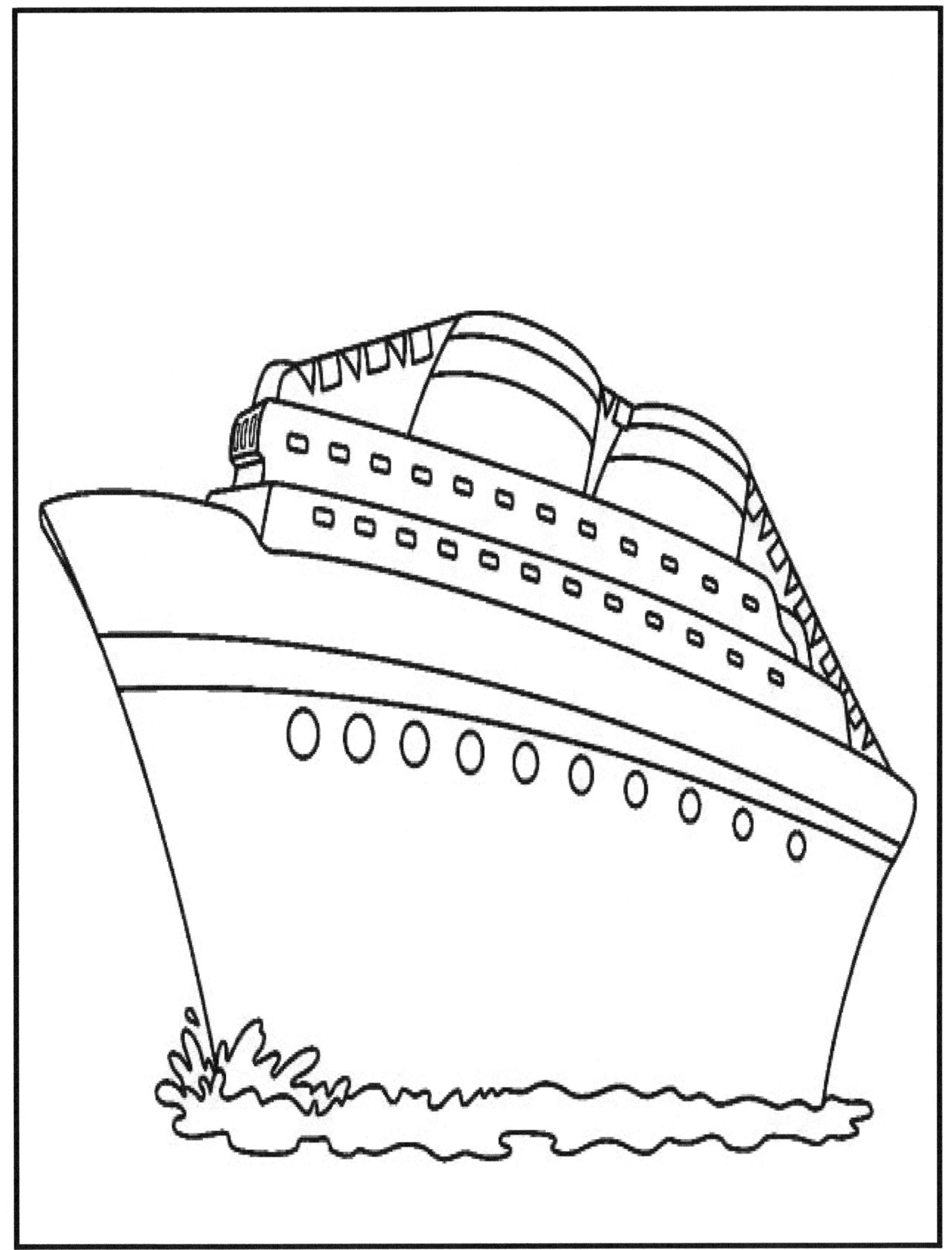

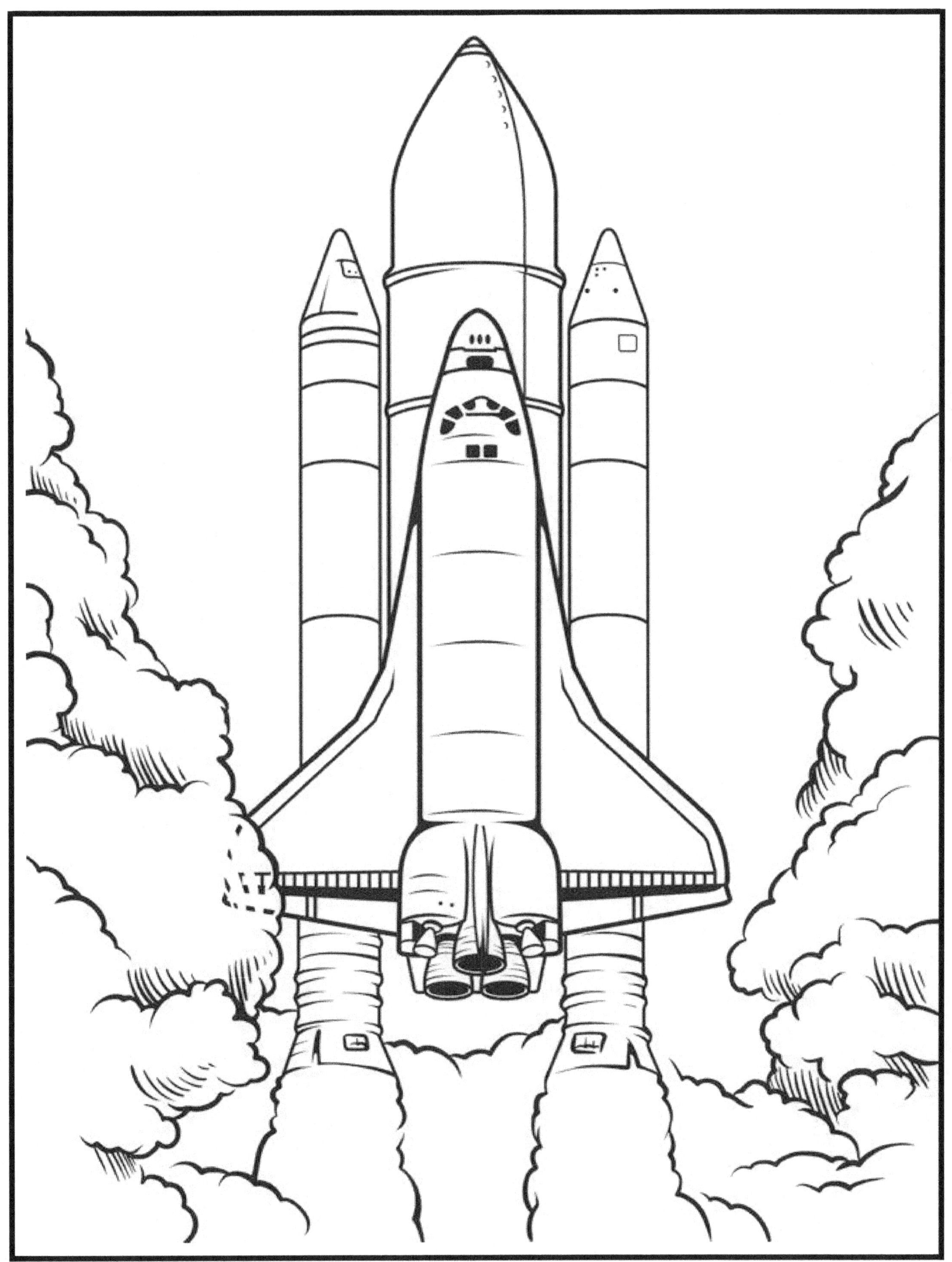

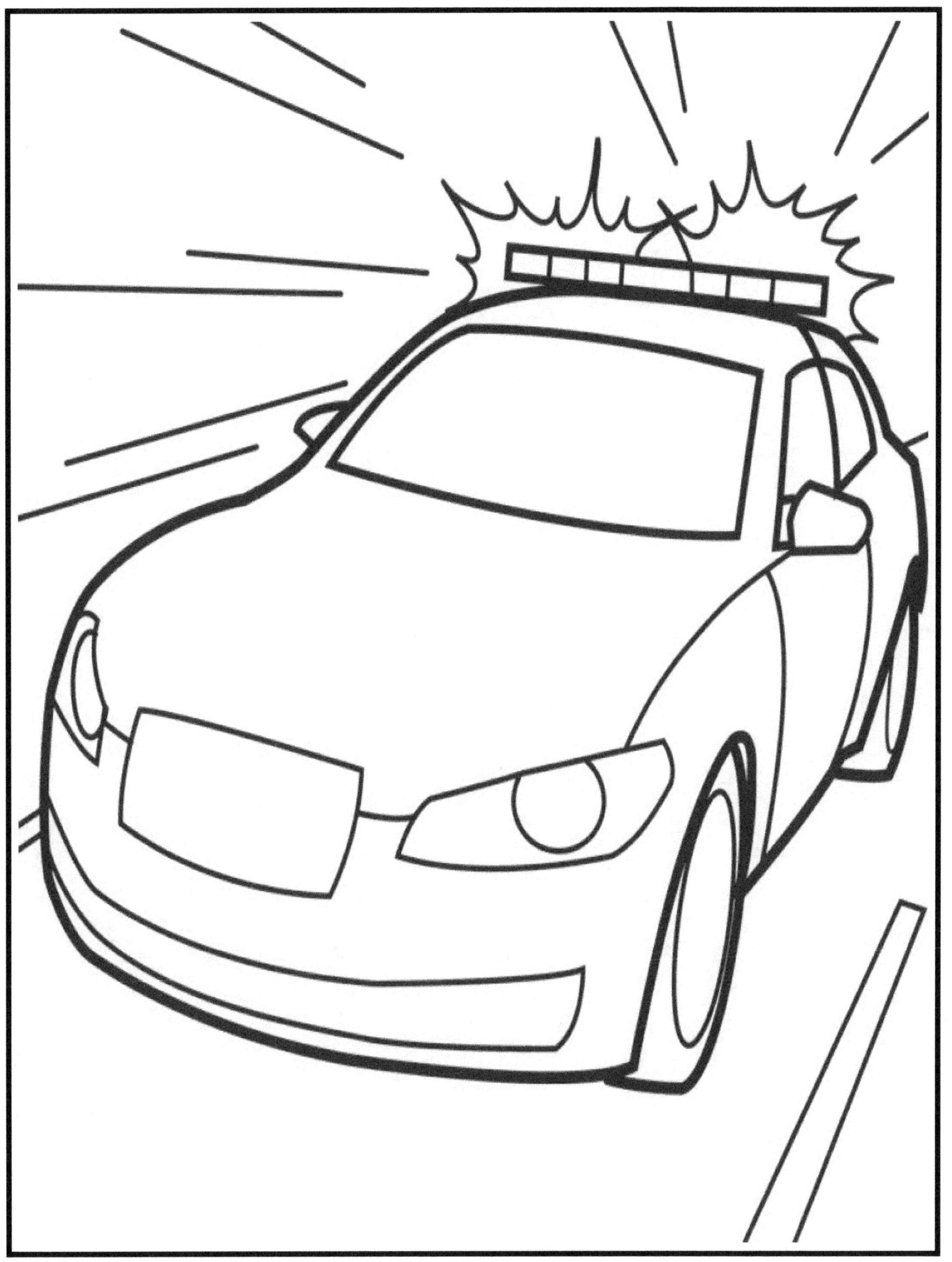

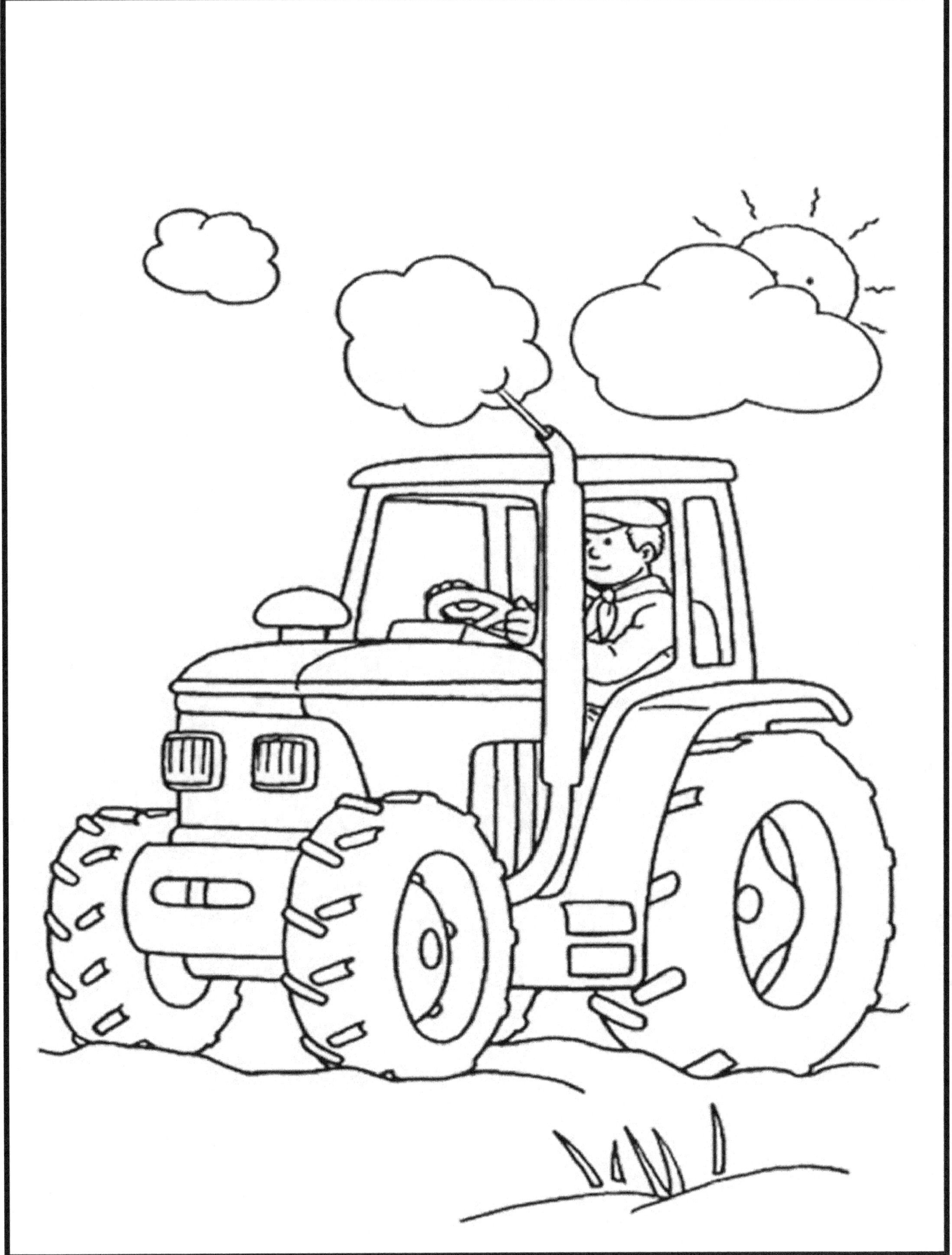

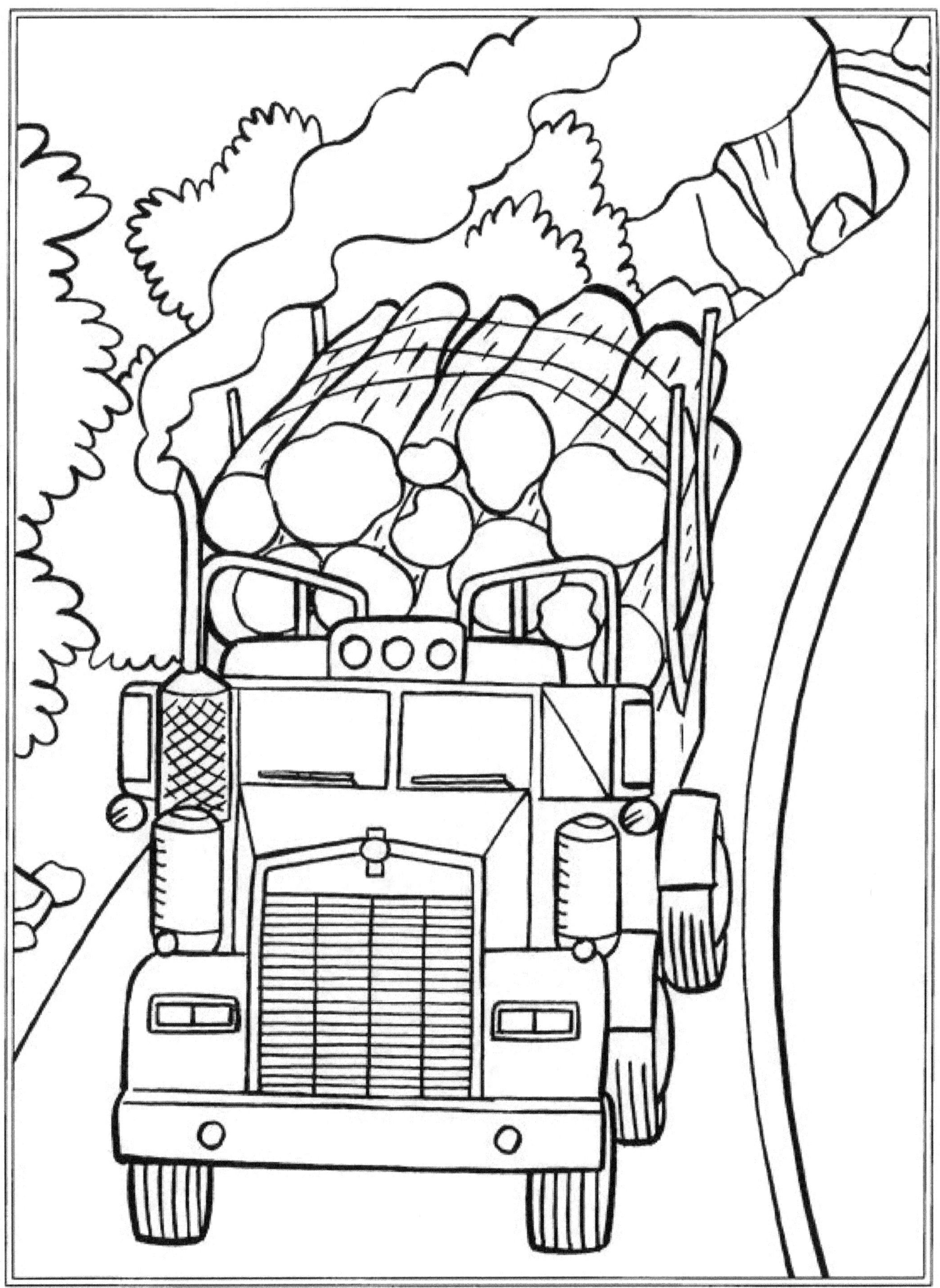

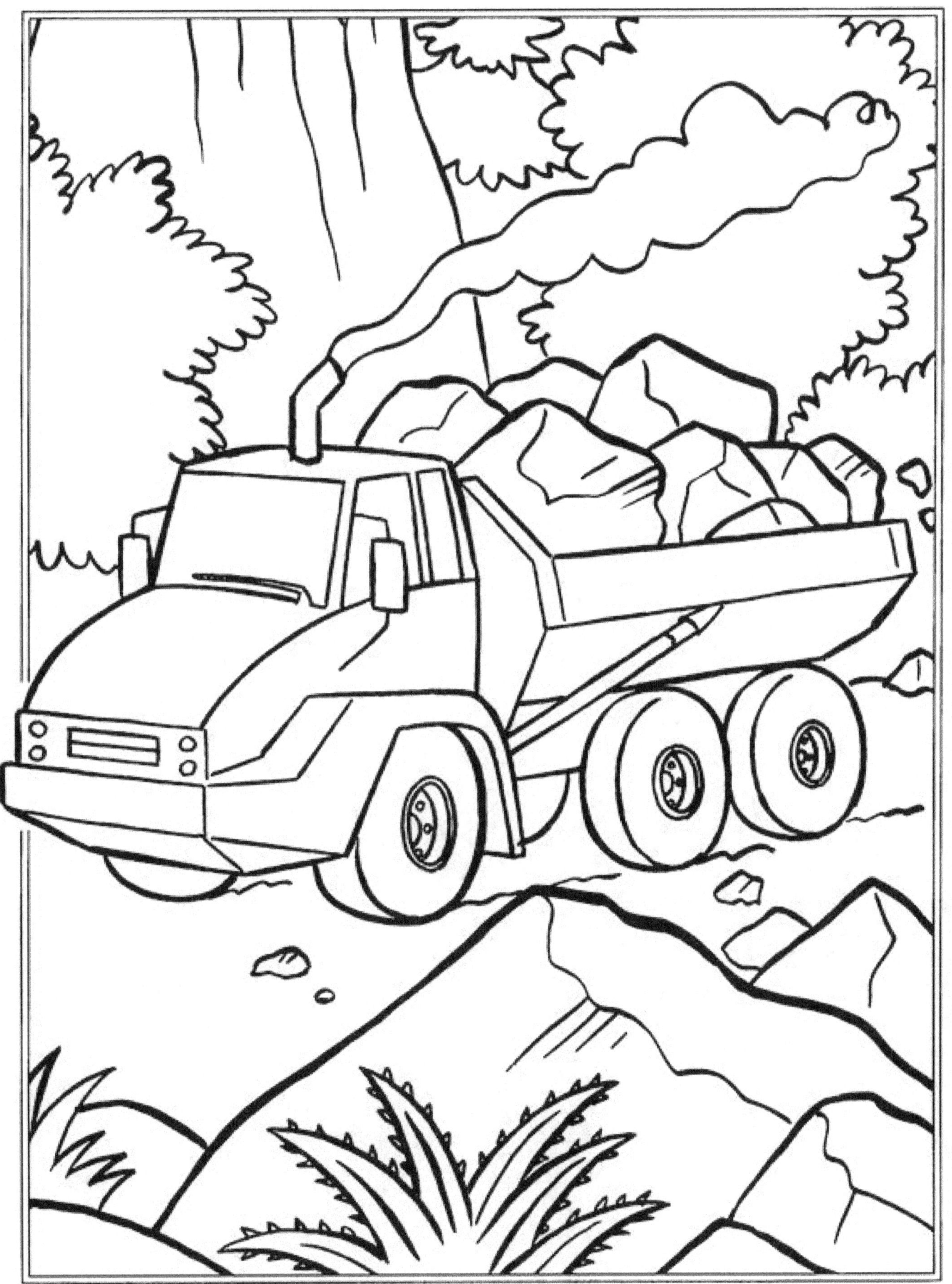

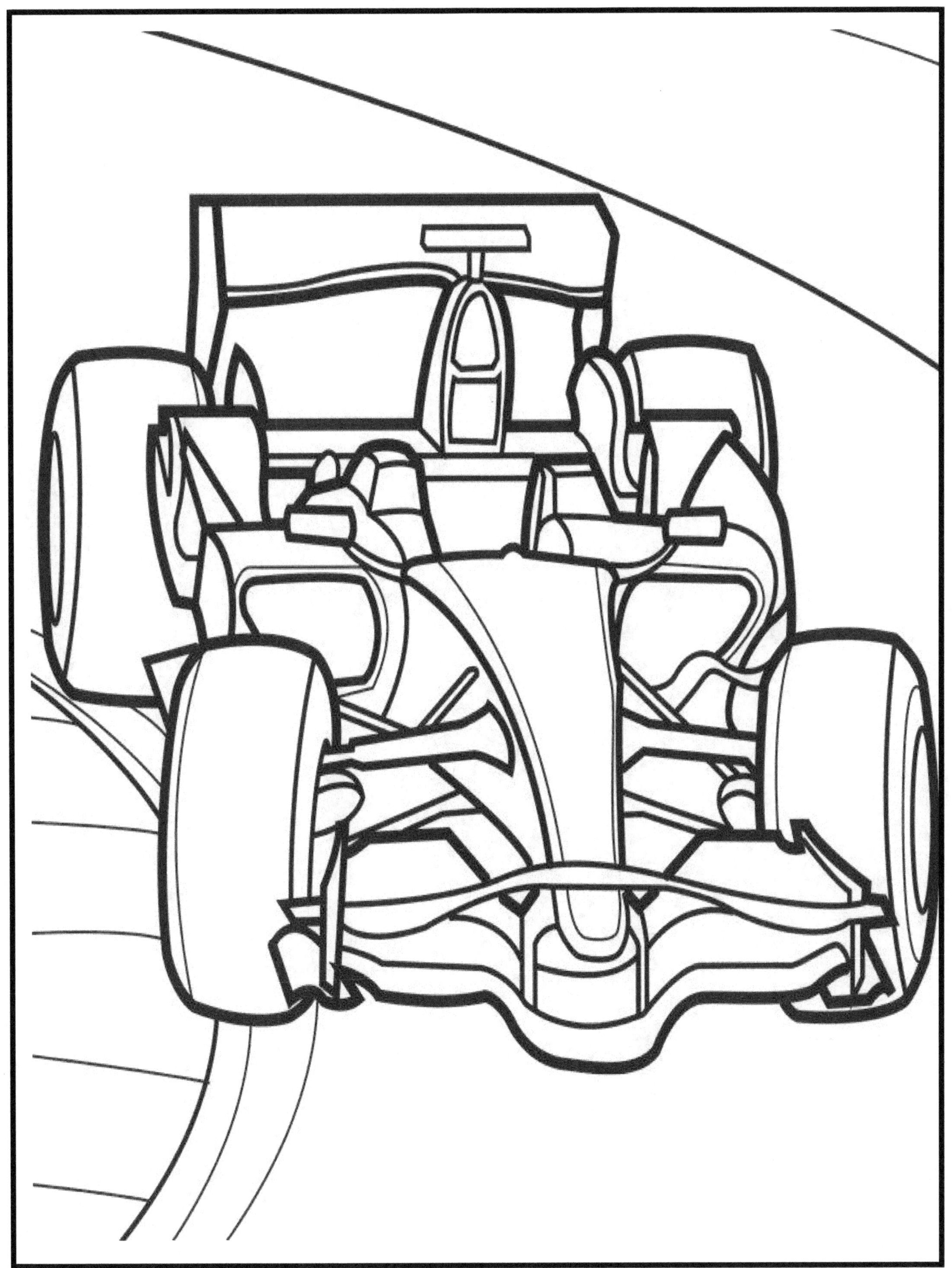

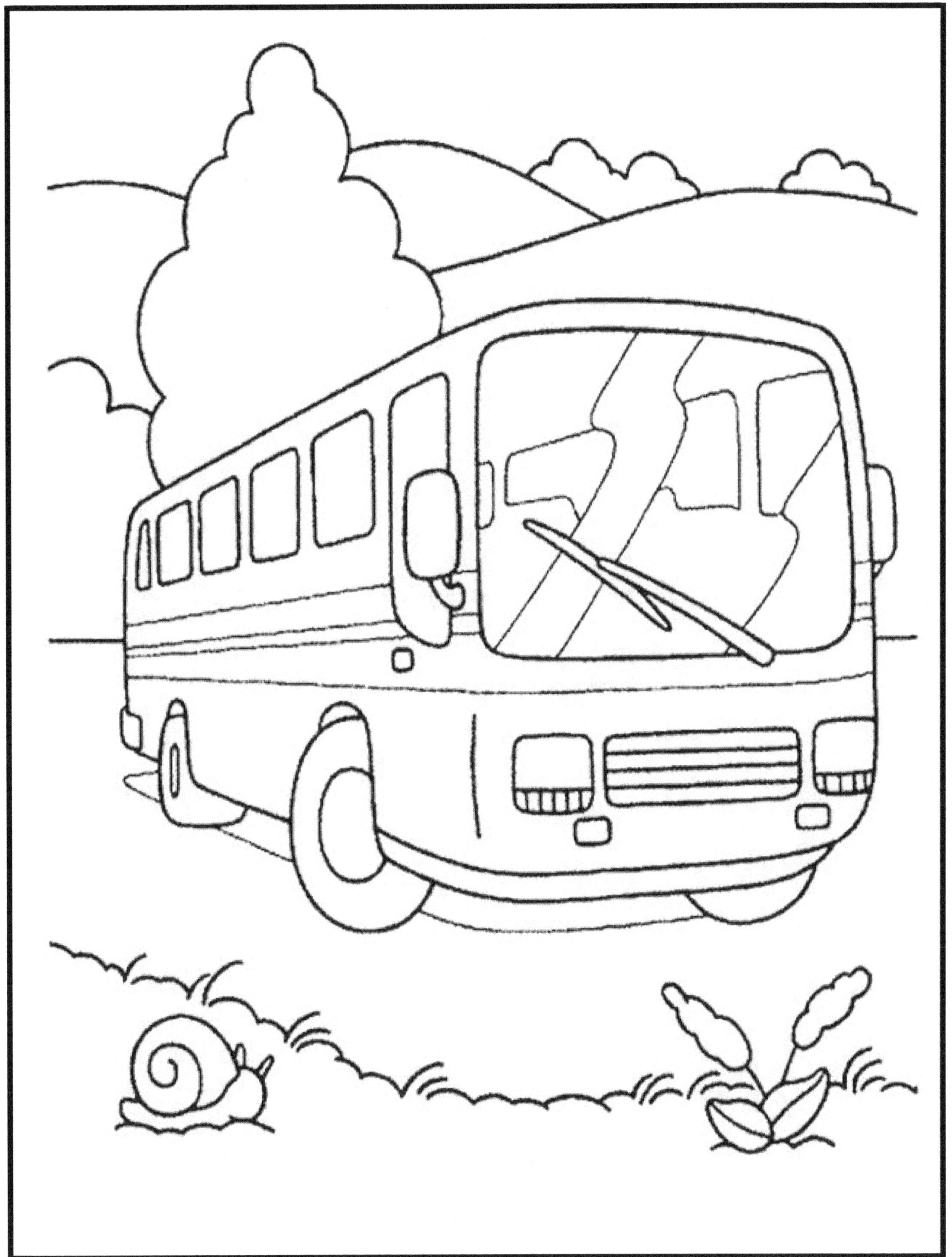

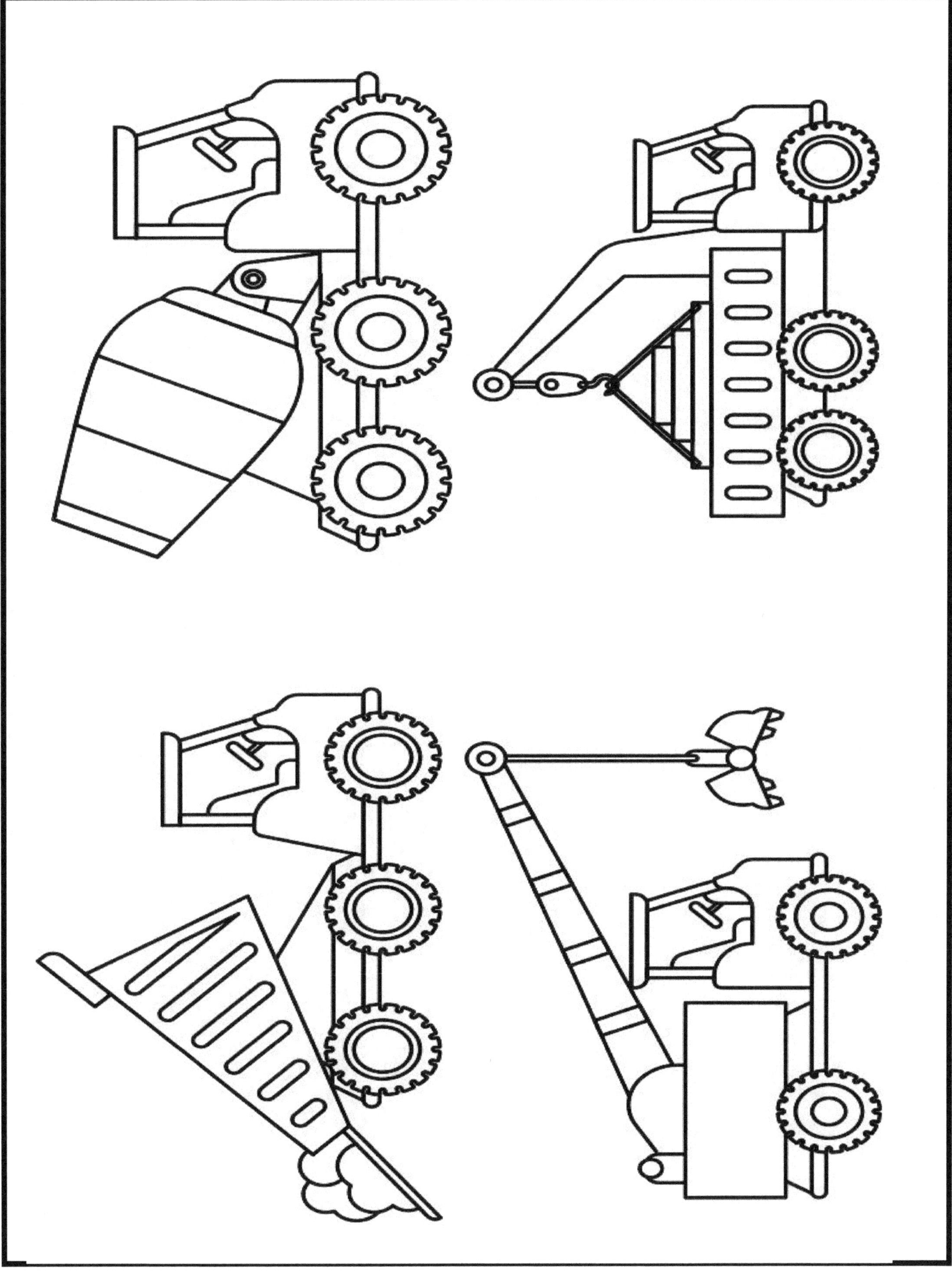

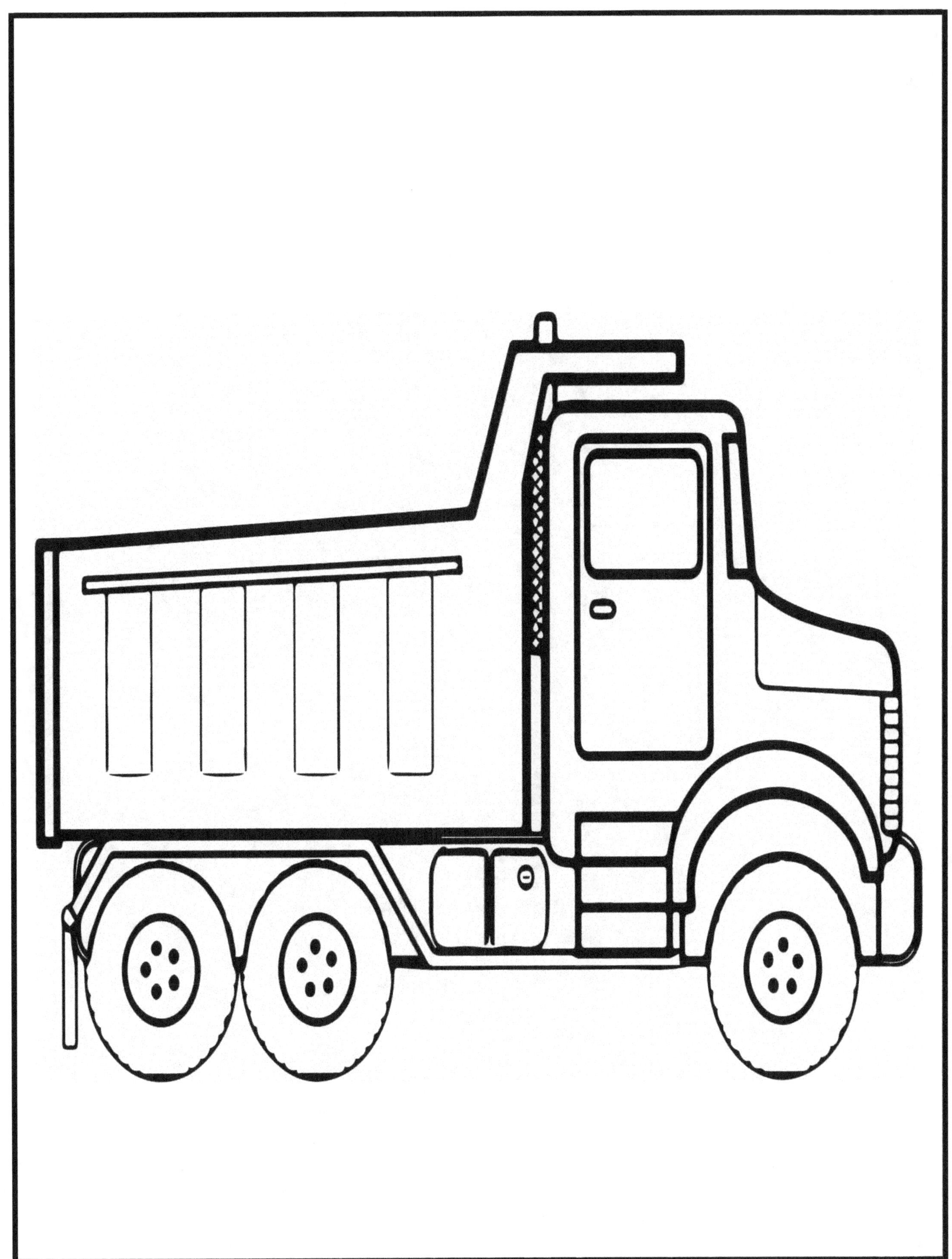

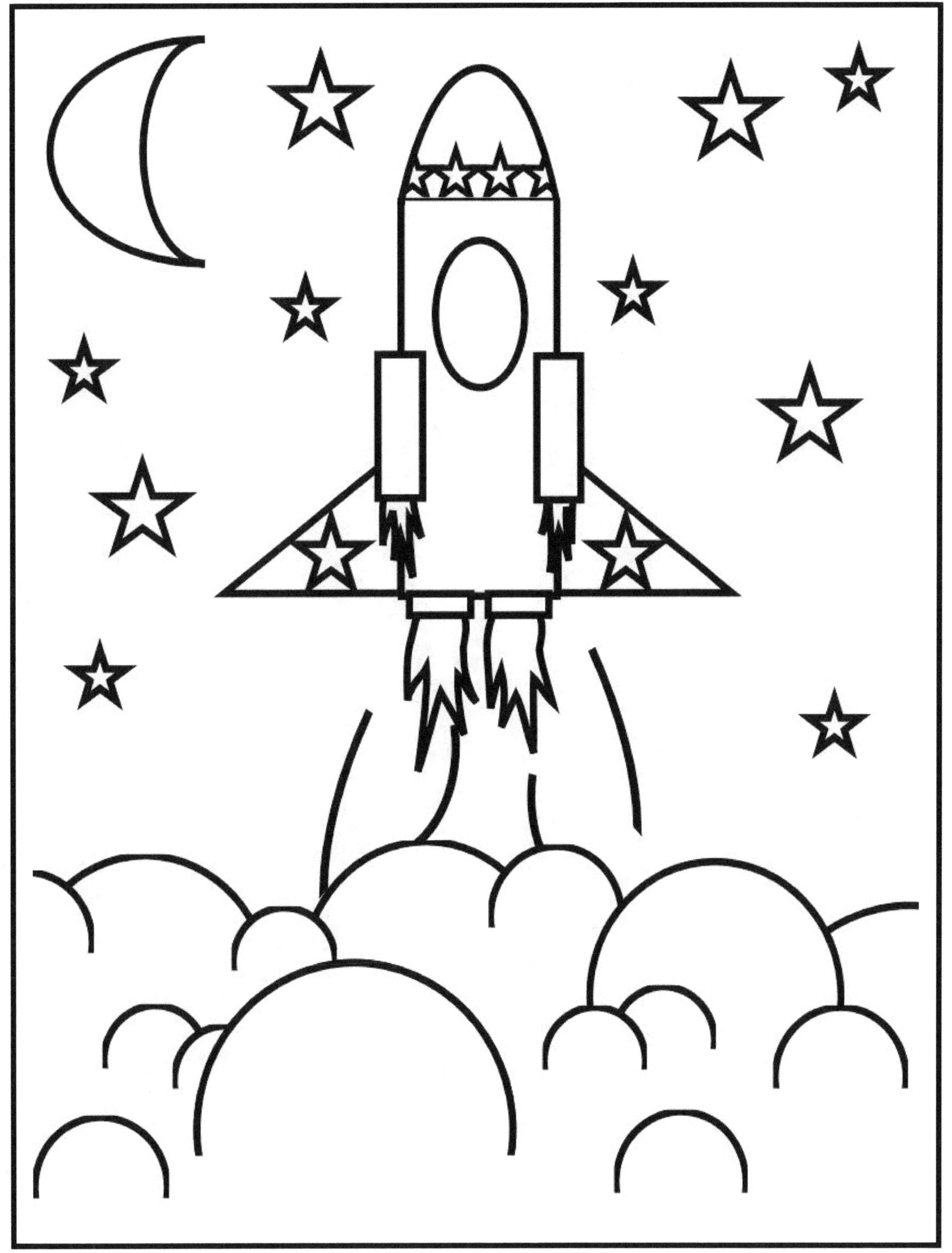

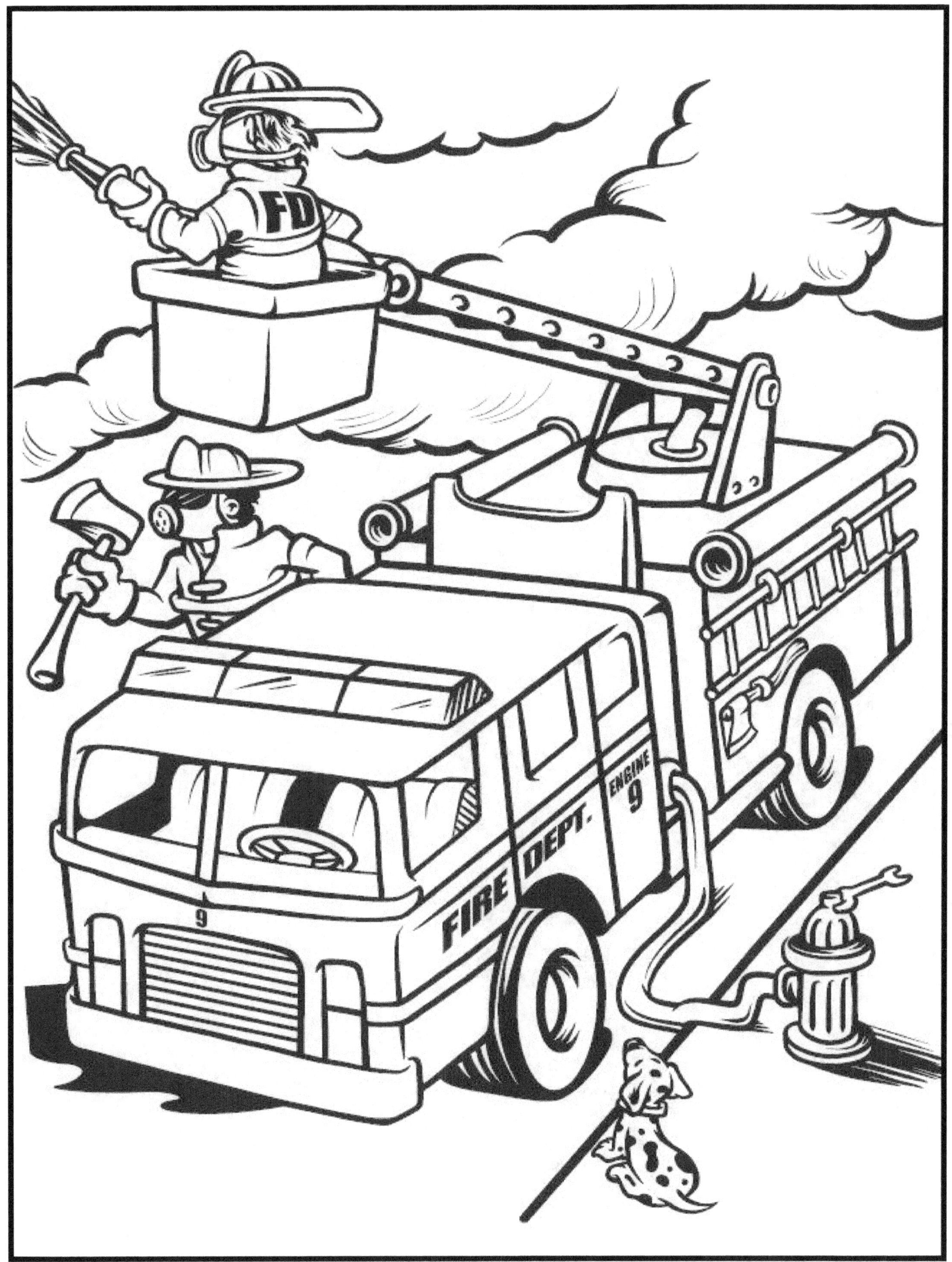

FD
FIRE DEPT.
ENGINE 9
9

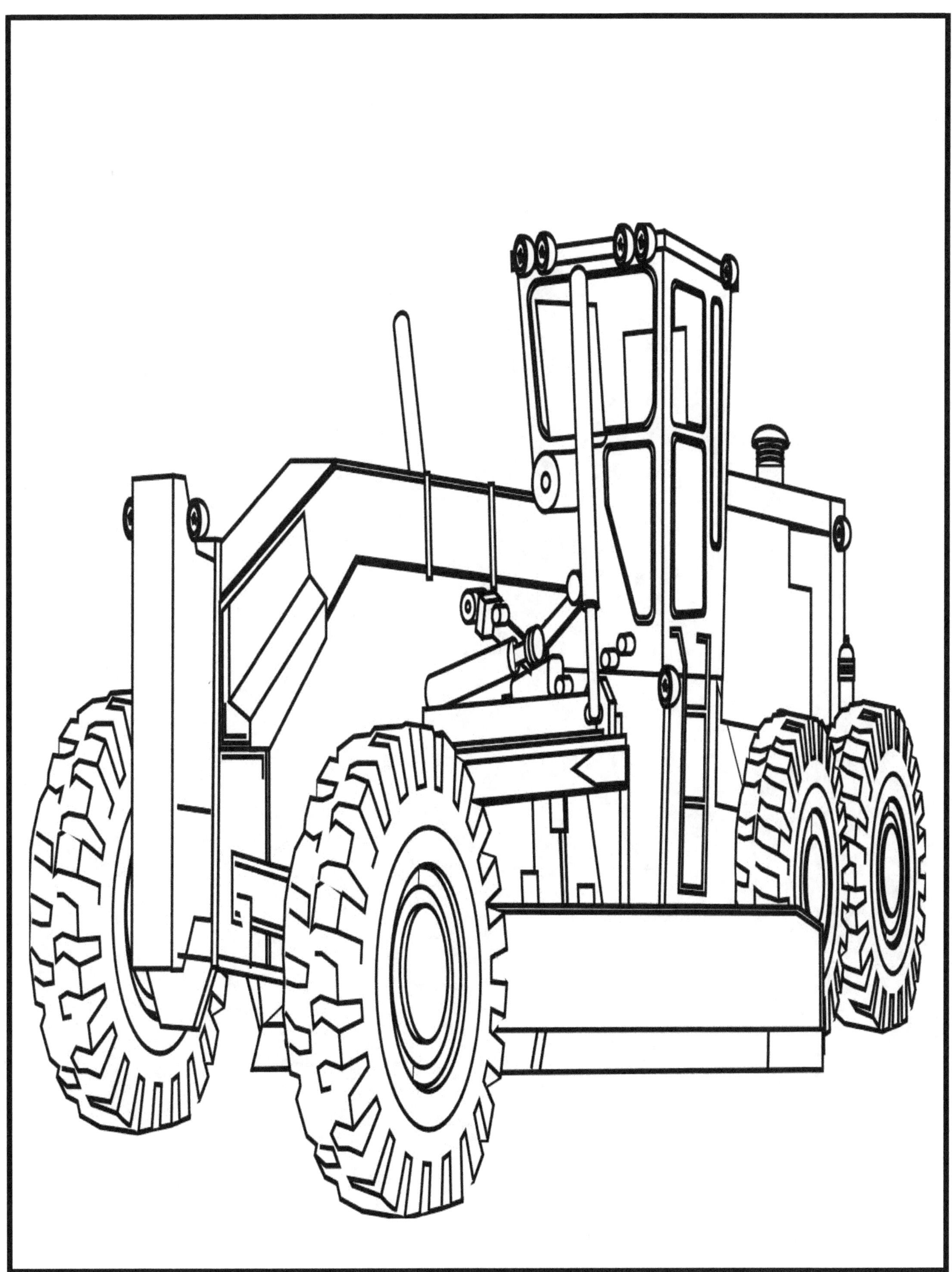

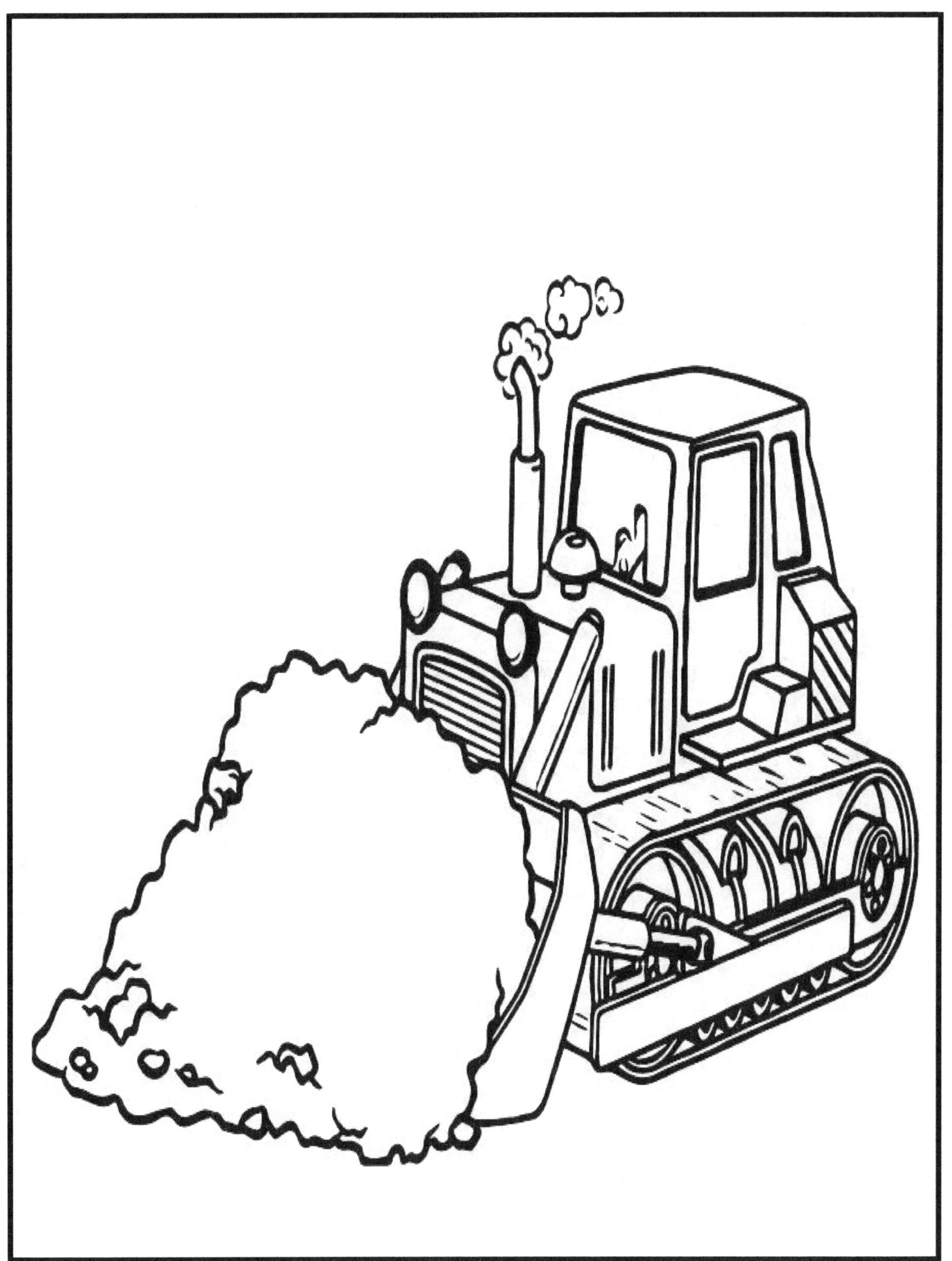

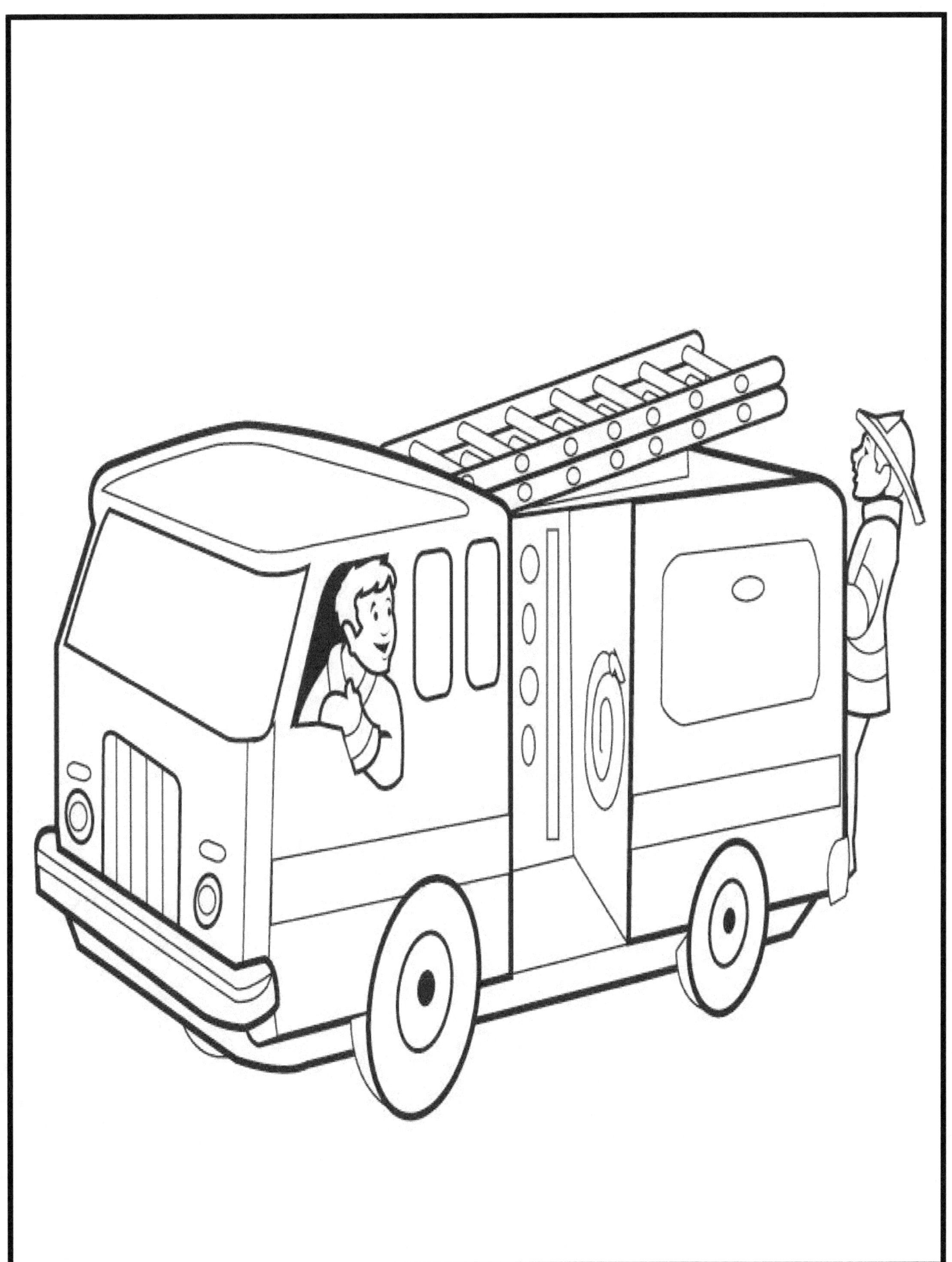

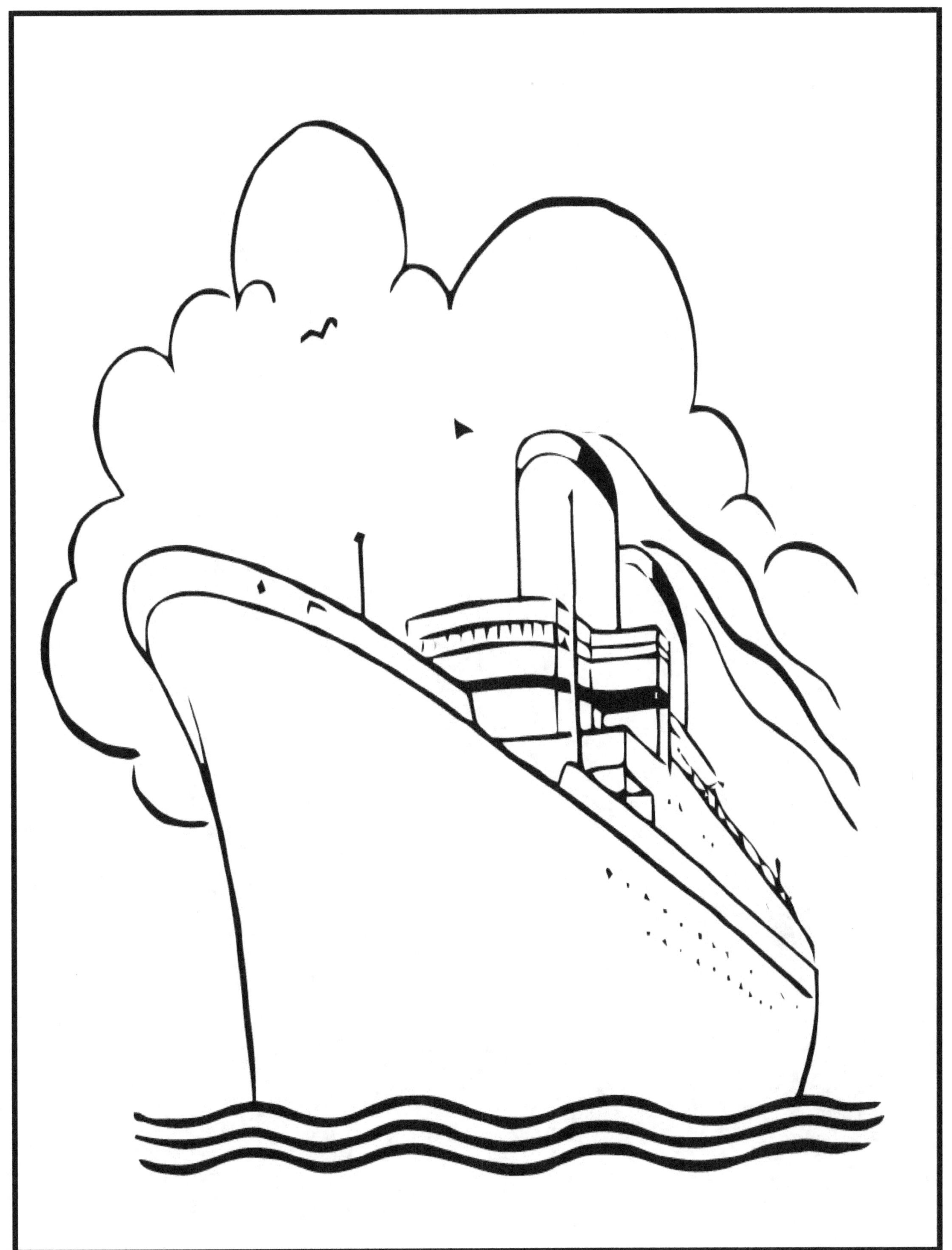

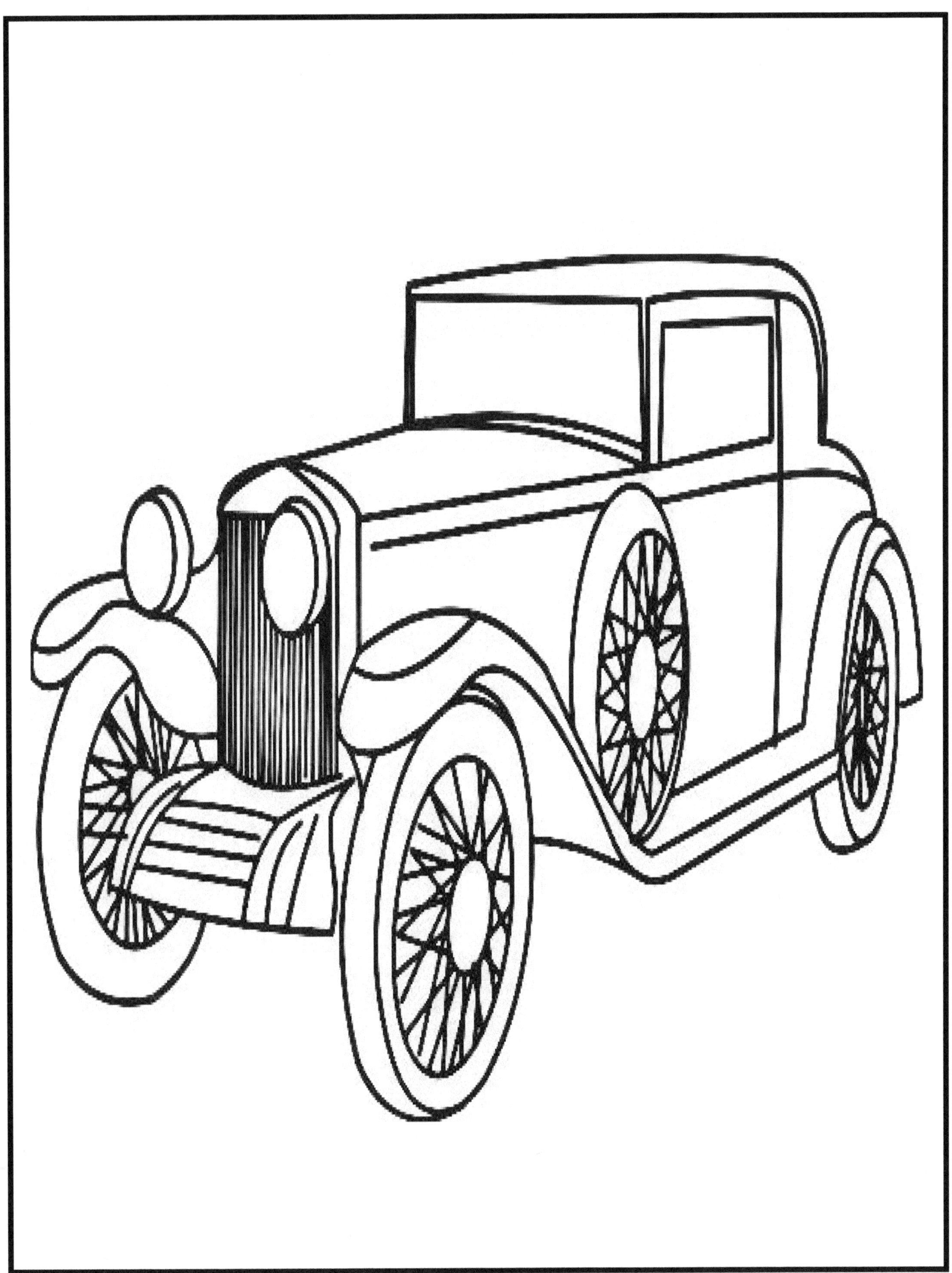

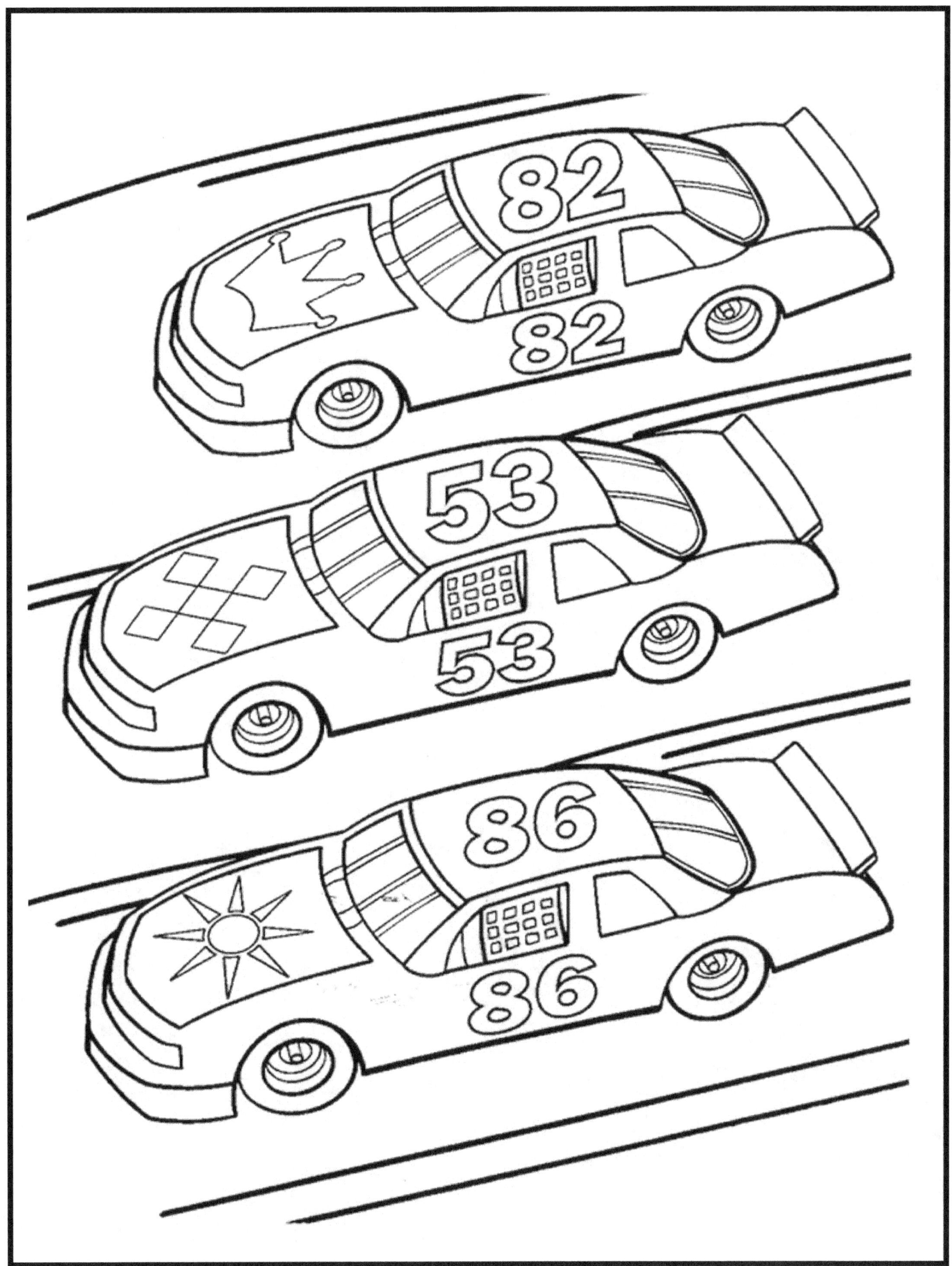
82
82
53
53
86
86

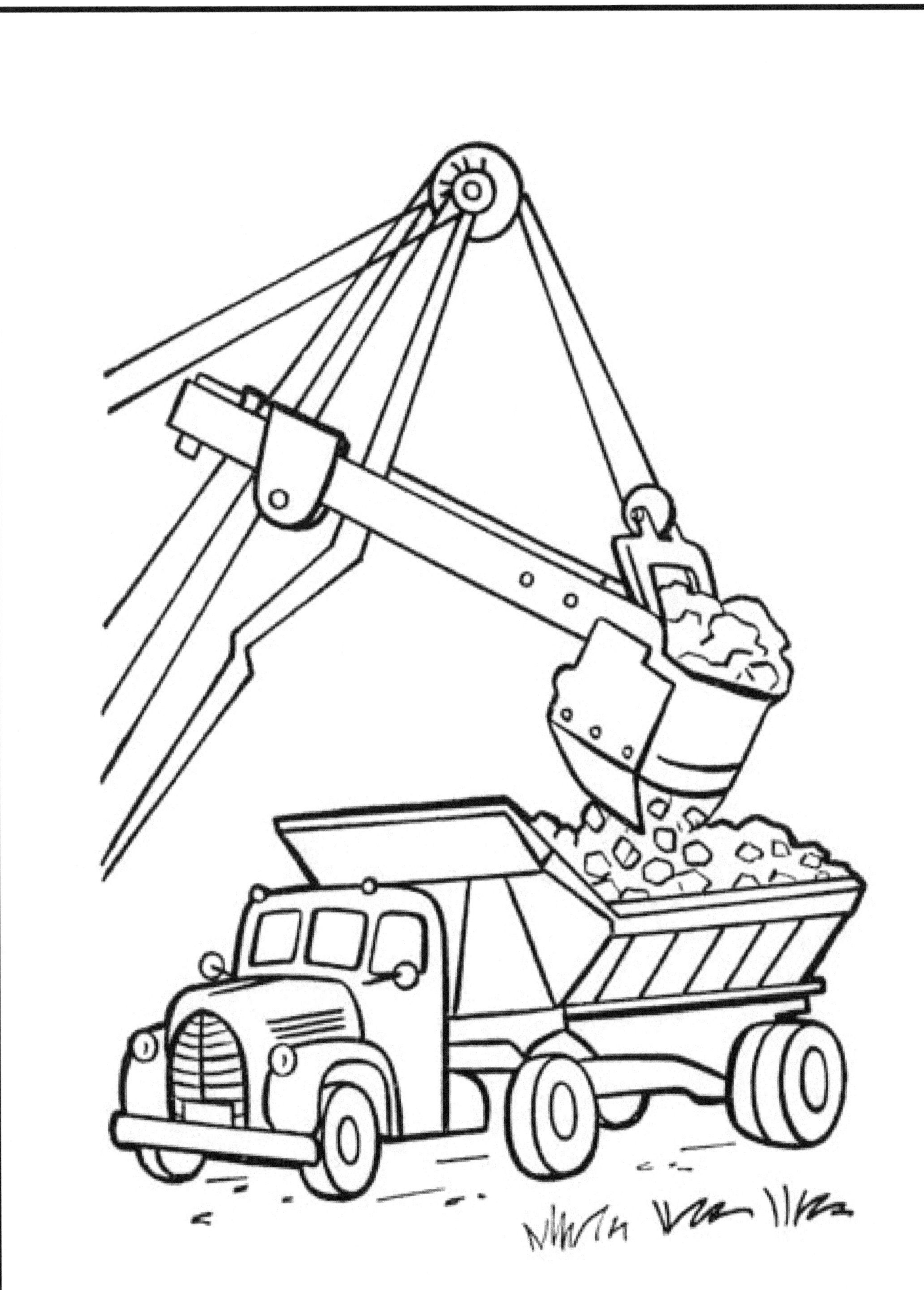

TEST COLORS